MILTON

ARISTOCRAT & REBEL

THE POET AND HIS POLITICS

MILTON

ARISTOCRAT & REBEL

THE POET AND HIS POLITICS

Perez Zagorin

D. S. BREWER

First published 1992 by D. S. Brewer

D. S. Brewer is an imprint of Boydell & Brewer Inc.
PO Box 41026, Rochester, New York 14604, USA
and PO Box 9, Woodbridge, Suffolk, IP12 3DF, UK

ISBN 0 85991 360 0

Library of Congress Cataloging-in-Publication Data
Zagorin, Perez.
　　　Milton : aristocrat & rebel : the poet and his politics /
Perez Zagorin.
　　　　　p.　　cm.
　　　Includes bibliographical references.
　　　ISBN 0-85991-360-0 (alk. paper)
　　　1. Milton, John, 1608–1674 – Political and social
views. 2. Politics and literature – England – History –
17th century. 3. Great Britain – Politics and government
– 1642–1660. 4. Political poetry, English – History and
criticism.　I. Title.
PR3592.P7Z33　1992
821′.4–dc20　　　　　　　　　　　　　　　　92-38015

British Library Cataloguing-in-Publication Data
Zagorin, Perez
　　　Milton: Aristocrat and Rebel – The Poet
and His Politics
　　　I. Title
　　　821.4
　　　ISBN 0-85991-360-0

This publication is printed on acid-free paper

Printed in the United States of America

CONTENTS

Give me the liberty to know, to utter, and to argue freely according to conscience, above all liberties.

Milton, *Areopagitica*

A man cannot make himself smaller than he is, and he cannot make himself different; a man creates what a man is, and all art is truth - the truth about the artist.

Thomas Mann, "The Sorrows And Grandeur of Richard Wagner," *Pro And Contra Wagner*

ABBREVIATIONS

CF *The Poems of John Milton*, edited by John Carey and Alistair Fowler (Longman: London, 1968)

CPW *Complete Prose Works of John Milton*, general editor Don M. Wolfe, 8 vols. in 10 (New Haven: Yale University Press, 1953–1982)

Parker William R. Parker, *Milton. A Biography*, 2 vols. (Oxford: Clarendon Press, 1968)

PREFACE

For three hundred years Milton has ranked as the second of English poets, and a huge body of writings has grown up about his life and work. Although for obvious reasons most of these writings have been dedicated to his poetry, literary scholars have also given close attention to his prose compositions, mainly in order to gain a better understanding of his beliefs and values for the light they can shed on his poems. Beside the limited treatment of Milton's politics in many literary studies, in biographies, and in various editions of his prose, a few works exist that are heavily concerned with his political thought. Of these probably the best known are Don M. Wolfe's *Milton and the Puritan Revolution* (1941), Arthur E. Barker's *Milton and the Puritan Dilemma 1641–1660* (1942), and Christopher Hill's *Milton and the English Revolution* (1978). Wolfe's book, a useful contribution at the time of its appearance, is by now rather outdated. Barker's study, while it continues to stand out in the Milton literature for its depth and insight, accorded a greater importance than is warranted to the poet's theological conceptions in shaping his political doctrines and idea of liberty. As for Hill's, the largest and most recent of these works, it is seriously flawed, I think, despite its author's great knowledge of Milton's time, by its crude political decodings of Milton's poetry and its inability to provide any evidence to sustain its novel central thesis that Milton developed his religious and political beliefs in a continuous dialogue with the lower class radical and fringe groups of his society. It has seemed to me, therefore, that there is at this date both room and a genuine need for a general modern account and examination of Milton's political philosophy set in the closest relationship to his intellectual and personal history and to his experience as a political man during the English revolution. To provide such an account is the purpose of this book.

Milton's personality and allegiances have always evoked strong and conflicting reactions from his readers. Some have disliked his revolutionary stand and religious principles, others have admired them. Dr Johnson, no lover of Milton, attributed his opposition to kings and prelates to envy, pride, and a hatred of obedience and authority. Shelley, on the other hand, praised "the sacred Milton" as a republican and bold inquirer into morals and religion. Macaulay likewise hailed him as the great poet and lofty patriot who stood in the forefront of the fight for liberty against despotism. Later authorities have given us equally differing images of Milton. Like Dr Johnson, T. S. Eliot in his famous essays on Milton's poetry did not conceal his distaste for the man and his beliefs. The revered Christian humanist that some Miltonists depict is by no means identical with the repressive moralist, the poet with little interest in individual human beings, the heretical Christian, or the ambivalent advocate of a wicked God that others present to us. As new trends in criticism have emerged, further diversities appear. Many recent feminist critics labor to convict Milton of sexism and misogyny, while others no less feminist defend him against these charges or even picture him as a feminist himself. Marxist and leftist scholars claim to recover the populist and revolutionary artist whom conservative critics have allegedly obscured or attempt to explain his thought as the reflection of an emergent bourgeois ideology.

A writer on Milton today, especially one who like myself is not a literary specialist but an intellectual, cultural, and political historian, does not find it easy to deal with current critical perspectives on the poet. Postmodernism, deconstruction, and the new historicism and its British variant, cultural materialism, which dominate literary studies at the present time, regard the text as involved with other texts in an endless play of intertextuality, construe it as self-subverting and riven with contradiction, dismiss the notion of authorial autonomy, intention, and integrity, and conceive the literary work not as a unique creative achievement but as a discursive product of its culture inscribed through and through by the culture's conflicted power relationships. Among the peculiar consequences of these views, in which the influence of Marxism and Foucault looms large, is that every text is held to be political and that no cultural domain can exist which is not political.

I have reflected on these critical positions, but have not found them persuasive. In the case of Milton, it seems to me impossible to deny him a significant measure of creative autonomy and integrity both as poet and publicist or to consider his work merely as a discursive product determined by his culture rather than as the highly individual creation that it was. Nor do I believe that it is possible to understand his political tracts without attending to his intention in writing them, the meaning he wanted to convey, and the end he hoped they would achieve. Although his writings harbor contradictions, they do not arise from the nature of language, as deconstructionists would argue, but from the insoluble dilemmas he confronted as a politically committed artist during the English revolution. Finally, since the indefinitely extended concept of the political which many contemporary literary scholars assume is to my mind more than doubtful, I have not been able to read Milton as if all his work were saturated with political meanings and issues of power. Except perhaps at certain times, politics and the political were not his predominant interest. Considerable parts of his poetry have nothing to do with politics or power in the proper sense. Moreover, as I hope this book will show, politics for him was generally less important than morals and always subservient to the latter.

Having said this, I should inform the reader that the following work is not concerned with theoretical issues and controversies in literary criticism; nor does it spend much time in trying to refute current arguments and opinions concerning Milton that I consider unfounded and erroneous. Instead, having thought about Milton and his work for a number of years, I have aimed to offer an independent account and appraisal of his politics. I have attempted to understand and follow Milton's mind in its political manifestations. In undertaking this task, I have done my best to avoid what has become a common failing in contemporary discussions of Milton, namely the intrusion and projection by authors of their own political wishes and allegiances into the interpretations of the poet's work.

This book is organized around Milton's relationship to the English revolution, the decisive event of his life and time. It is the revolution in its external and internal conflicts at its successive stages that constitutes the fundamental context of his political reflection and activity. At the same time, however, the connection between his public activity and ideas and his personal history was so close that I have found it essential to relate the movement of his thought to the facts of his biography. His psychology, his character, and his conception of himself were crucial in defining his political convictions. If we fail to understand or take them into account, we cannot really understand him as a political man. I have begun with an examination of his earlier self-formation in adolescence and youth, since this was so vital to what he conceived his role as poet and publicist to be when he became politically engaged in the conflict against the Stuart monarchy. I have then traced his political course as a revolutionary and republican and surveyed his successive writings and the evolution of his political theory and opinions during the twenty years of the revolution. After this, I have sought to ascertain where he stood and what survived of his convictions following the

Restoration, which extinguished his last remaining hopes and made him something like an exile in his own country. Finally, I have concluded with a retrospect and summary of Milton's political philosophy. Throughout my study I have endeavored to show that the principle of aristocracy linked to virtue constituted a predominant element in the rebel Milton's political thought which helps to explain many of his enduring attitudes.

Anyone who would write about Milton incurs an immense debt of gratitude to the erudition and insight of the scholars, editors, and critics who have added so much to the understanding of his life, art, and thought. I have benefited from their knowledge to a much greater extent than my notes indicate. In the latter I have usually followed the rule of citing from my reading only those works directly pertinent to the subjects I have discussed or immediately related to some particular point under consideration. Readers wishing to acquaint themselves with the body of important literature devoted to Milton in the twentieth century will find it helpful, as I have, to consult *The Essential Milton: An Annotated Bibliography of Milton Studies*, ed. P. J. Klemp (Boston: G. K. Hall, 1989), which contains over a thousand entries, as well as M. A. Mikolaczak's bibliographical essay in *The Cambridge Companion to Milton*, ed. Dennis Danielson (Cambridge: Cambridge Univerasity Press, 1989). For biographical details and much else, I have relied on William R. Parker's full and painstaking biography of Milton, the only real successor to Masson's great nineteenth-century life of the poet. Whenever the following pages mention any facts concerning Milton without specific documentation, they are derived from Parker's biography. References to Milton's poetry are based on the edition of his poems by John Carey and Alistair Fowler; to Milton's prose writings, on the now completed Yale edition.

This book is dedicated to the memory of my Harvard teacher and friend, W. K. Jordan, whose monumental work on the development of religious toleration in England from the Reformation to 1660 first introduced me to the rich literature in behalf of the cause of which Milton is the most famous champion.

Chapter 1

BEFORE THE REVOLUTION:
MILTON'S SELF-FORMATION

The following essay presents a study of Milton's political thought and beliefs in the light of his personal and political history and experiences. Although it discusses Milton's poetry, it does so chiefly with the aim of elucidating his basic principles and values, not as a venture in literary criticism. Milton was not an original thinker or philosopher. If it were not for the fact that he was a very great artist, his political ideas would possess considerably less interest than they do and hardly justify the amount of attention scholars have given them. They are of very considerable interest, however, not only because they were his and deeply revealing of his character, but because they represent the response of a powerful mind, supreme poet, and politically committed intellectual to the foremost issues of his time, an era of crisis in which revolution temporarily overthrew England's inherited political and ecclesiastical order.

Milton was not driven by metaphysical perplexities and his politics were not the product of profound philosophic reflection in a rigorous search for truth. Most of his conceptions in the realm of political theory derived from others, but they were strongly colored by the intensity of his own convictions, needs, and imagination as he absorbed them into himself. They became thoroughly impregnated by his personality, from which his work whether as a publicist or poet remains wholly inseparable. Into whatever Milton wrote, and certainly in his prose treatises concerned with public and political affairs, he poured the same distinctive self. Without a clear insight into the nature of his personality, his enormous pride and ambition, his refusal ever to acknowledge inconsistency, error, or failure, and his constant will towards self-construction and self-mastery, neither his poetic achievement nor his political ideas can be understood.[1]

[1] In focusing this chapter upon Milton's self-formation, I have not had in mind the conception set forth in Stephen Greenblatt's influential book, *Renaissance Self-*

Milton was absolutely unique among all the English poets of his time and earlier in the quantity of documents he left describing his self-development and aspirations. No writer before him prepared himself so self-consciously and determinedly for the vocation of poetry or pursued more exalted hopes and aims as an artist. No other writer confided his hopes and aims so fully and candidly to his readers. Partly in some of his early letters and compositions, but especially in several of his subsequent prose writings, he reviewed his personal history, affirmed his fundamental values, and disclosed his grandiose literary and intellectual goals. These passages of deliberate confession and self-exposure sometimes occur in self-justification as a reply to criticism, sometimes gratuitously, without any logical necessity. Always, however, they betray an essential truth about Milton. They tell us not only what he was but what he wished to be, how he perceived himself and how he wished to be perceived by others. They also furnish essential evidence concerning the roots of his enduring moral and political attitudes.

Milton's life falls into three broadly defined periods. The first, from his birth on 9 December 1608 to the outbreak of the revolt against the Stuart monarchy in 1640, includes his education at St Paul's School and Christ's College, Cambridge, the six years thereafter of his private studies between 1632 and 1638, and his European journey in 1638–39. This period saw the composition of his first important poems, notably the *Nativity Ode* (1629), *Comus* (1634), and *Lycidas* (1637), works stamped by the highest promise of future achievement. At this time too he formed his idealistic

Fashioning from More to Shakespeare (Chicago: University of Chicago Press, 1980). Greenblatt treats the fashioning of the self as a specifically Renaissance phenomenon. He associates it with certain social and psychological conditions including submission to an absolute power or authority situated outside the self, and believes that it was achieved in relation to an alien, threatening, and external Other; (introduction and pp. 8–9). This account, which rests on some dubious historical assumptions such as the claim that personal autonomy probably declined in the sixteenth century, would not apply well to Milton, nor do I refer here to his self-formation in this sense. Rather, I mean to describe by it the struggle many creative spirits must wage against discordant inner impulses, desires, and aims, which the self strives to sublimate, order, and overcome so as to perform the demanding tasks it aspires to accomplish. In the case of Milton one cannot avoid adding that the feeling he expressed for the self he formed by his disciplined life was so reverential that it seems at time to have bordered on self-worship. Richard Helgerson, *Self-Crowned Laureates* (Berkeley: University of California Press, 1983), deals with the personal beliefs of Spenser, Jonson, Milton, and other authors concerning the role of the poet in the context of their own society's attitude on the subject, but does not discuss Milton's self-development.

conception of the poet as a God-inspired prophet and teacher of nations which became the guiding motif of his life.

The second period, from 1640 to 1660, comprises the beginning of the English revolution, the civil war and parliament's victory over Charles I, the establishment of the commonwealth or republic, the Cromwellian protectorate, and the revolution's final failure and collapse as the victim of its own dissensions. Stirred to the depths by the struggle, Milton was a committed participant from the outset, producing little poetry during these years and devoting a large part of his energies to pamphleteering in behalf of the revolutionary cause. In 1649 he accepted office under the commonwealth as its secretary for foreign correspondence. Of the two dozen or so tracts belonging to this time, the ones that gained him the widest contemporary renown were his defenses of the deposition and execution of the king, the republican regime, and the rule of Oliver Cromwell. In 1652, partly as the result of his labors as a propagandist, he became totally blind. The beginning of the composition of *Paradise Lost* probably dates from the latter part of this period.

The third period extends from the restoration of the monarchy in 1660 to his death in 1674. Milton was endangered by the restoration and might even have been executed for his political past. He was forced to go into hiding, was imprisoned in the Tower for several weeks, and his works were burnt. Through the influence of friends and well wishers, though, he was released and thereafter left unmolested. His greatest works appeared during this last period, *Paradise Lost* in 1667, *Paradise Regained* and *Samson Agonistes* in 1671.

Throughout his career, from at least late adolescence onward, Milton conceived greatness and immortality as a poet as his aim and destiny. His history may thus be read as a continual process of the formation of personality towards that end, combined with unremitting determination to repel and cancel the interior forces of doubt, self-division, and guilt that might compromise his self-conception. In the course of his life as outlined above, he experienced three major crises that posed a severe threat to his vision of himself. The first, a consequence of his hasty marriage in 1642 to Mary Powell, a girl sixteen years younger than himself of a Royalist family, was the shock of his wife's leaving him after only a few weeks together. Keenly humiliated by her desertion and his poor choice of a spouse, he was forced to contend with a fierce blow to his self-esteem. The second crisis was the calamity of his blindness which struck him in 1652. As a devoutly religious man, he could not escape the thought that his loss of sight might be a direct punishment on him from God

3

for some offense. The third crisis was the inglorious end of the English revolution and return of kingship in 1660. A republican and political idealist, Milton was at first inspired by the revolution, but became increasingly disillusioned as it progressed. The shock of the Restoration compelled him to reappraise his political principles and to consider whether providence had not rejected the cause for which he fought. As this study proceeds, we shall need to look at the manner in which he responded to each of these grave adversities that threatened his self-integration and belief.

Milton was born the older son of a prosperous London family. His mother, Sara Jeffrey, was the daughter of a London merchant-tailor. Although he expresses a dutiful admiration of her virtues, he says almost nothing else about her in his writings. His father, John Milton senior, was the son of an Oxfordshire yeoman who remained loyal to Catholicism after England became a Protestant state under Queen Elizabeth. Disinherited and forced to leave home because he embraced Protestantism, the elder Milton migrated to London about 1582 at the age of twenty. There he became apprenticed to a scrivener, an occupation involving the drafting of legal and commercial documents and the functions of receiving money on deposit, acting as broker between lender and borrower, and making loans at interest. In this profession, which offered many opportunities to a shrewd business intelligence, Milton's father prospered, thus gaining, wrote Edward Phillips, Milton's nephew and contemporary biographer, "a competent estate whereby he was enabled to make a handsome Provision both for the Education and Maintenance of his Children...."[2] Referring to his comfortable financial circumstances, Milton later expressed his gratitude to providence,

> who hath ever bred me up in plenty, although my life hath not bin unexpensive in learning, and voyaging about, so long as it shall please him to lend mee what he hath hitherto thought good, which is anough to serve me in all honest and liberall occasions, and something over besides....[3]

Aside from his business interests, Milton's father was also an accomplished musician as well as composer. Although he probably never attended a university, he may as a boy have been a chorister at

---

[2] Edward Phillips, *The Life of Mr. John Milton*, printed in Helen Darbishire, *The Early Lives of Milton* (London: Constable, 1932), pp. 51–52.

[3] *An Apology against A Pamphlet*, 1642, CPW, vol. I, p. 929.

Christ Church, Oxford, which would help explain his musical training.

The most notable feature of John Milton's childhood and youth was the way his parents nurtured his extraordinary gifts and promise. The oldest of three siblings, he was made conscious very early that he was an exceptional being of whom much was expected. His preliminary education close to home at St Paul's School, which he probably entered at twelve if not sooner, equipped him with a strong foundation in the Greek and Latin languages in which he was to acquire such rich erudition. Beside his formal schooling his father also provided private tutors for him in French, Italian, Hebrew, and other subjects. He later recorded that his father had destined him in early childhood for the study of literature – by which must be understood the secular learning suitable for the ministry, not a professional career as a writer – and that from the age of twelve he scarcely ever left his studies for bed before midnight.[4] He also received a thorough religious training. The Milton household was under the spiritual direction of a parish clergyman who was one of the pillars of the London Puritan ministry, and it was accustomed to conscientious sabbath observance and sermon-going. The influences of home and school alike thus combined to imbue Milton with firmly founded religious convictions of a Puritan cast, including a strong animosity to Catholicism. Among his first compositions, done at fifteen, were English verse paraphrases of several of the psalms. It is important to emphasize, however, that while he rated his Protestant Christian faith as his highest and dearest possession, he never felt any conflict between it and his love of pagan or secular literature. The humanistic classical culture his father made possible for him seems always to have accommodated itself easily in a harmonious synthesis with his religious beliefs.

At fifteen Milton entered Cambridge, where he spent the next seven years as a member of Christ's College. He looked down upon the abilities of his fellow students, most of whom, like himself, were preparing for the ministry, and was not greatly popular among them. His dignity was affronted by a quarrel with his tutor, for which he was punished by suspension for a term. Although reading a great deal and taking part in the prescribed academic exercises, he was critical of the teaching methods and contemptuous of the arid scholastic philosophy he was obliged to learn. The impression he gives at this time is that of an independent, proud young man with a high estimate of himself, aloof and somewhat isolated, eager for the

---

[4] *A Second Defence of The People of England*, 1654, CPW, vol. IV, pt. 1, p. 612.

recognition of his fellows while holding himself above most of them. Apart from one close friend with whom he could share his thoughts, Charles Diodati, a former classmate at St Paul's who was then at Oxford, he had no companions or intimates. He probably lived a good deal in imagination with the English and classical poets and philosophers like Plato whose works inspired him so deeply.

Milton was twenty-four when he left Cambridge with an M. A. degree in 1632. Although planning to enter the ministry in accord with his father's wishes, he did not yet seek ordination or proceed on a career. Instead, he spent the next six years in further study. By now his father, nearing seventy, had retired from business, and Milton lived with his family, which moved to the London suburb of Hammersmith and then to the rural village of Horton in Buckinghamshire. During this time, which was given over partly to poetry but mostly to a systematic program of reading in a vast range of authors and subjects, he seems to have abandoned his intention to become a clergyman. In the spring of 1638, again enabled by his father's generosity, he embarked on a tour of the continent. Accompanied by a servant, he passed through France to Italy, the highlight of his journey. For him Italy was "the home of humane studies and of all the arts of civilization,"[5] and in Florence, Rome, and Naples he became friends with eminent men and writers who welcomed him as a distinguished foreigner, scholar, and gifted poet. Despite his dislike of the Catholicism he witnessed, he always treasured his Italian experiences, carrying back with him glowing memories of his reception and the associations he had made there. In the summer of 1639 he set out on his return, recalled, as he explained much later, by the tidings of civil war in England and thinking it base to travel abroad for the cultivation of his mind while his countrymen fought at home for liberty.[6] While this was his sentiment in retrospect, it could hardly have figured much at the time to which he referred; for although in 1639 Scotland was already in revolt against Charles I, England was still quiescent despite its disaffection and the civil war lay three years away.

These were some of the main circumstances of Milton's outward life as he passed from childhood through youth and into manhood beyond the age of thirty. Inwardly his evolution was marked by soaring ambition and consciousness of the rigorous preparation needed to make himself worthy of the vocation of poet. His sense of

[5] Ibid., p. 609.
[6] Ibid., p. 619.

6

consecration is already manifest in his *Sixth Elegy*, a Latin poem addressed at Christmas 1629 to his friend Diodati. Although laced with humor and high spirits, it also describes in a serious vein the strict morals and unspotted purity required of the poet who would write of gods and heroes. Such a poet, Milton says,

> Is sacred to the gods, and is their priest,
> His inmost heart and his mouth are both full of Jove.   (77–78)

In *On The Morning of Christ's Nativity*, an ode written at the same time, he alludes in immediately personal terms to the poet's prophetic function when picturing himself offering his poem as a gift to the newborn Christ as one whose voice joins the choir of angels from out God's "secret altar touched with hallowed fire." (27). This line echoes the biblical passage which describes an angel touching the prophet Isaiah's lips with a burning coal from God's altar as a sign of his prophetic inspiration. (Isaiah 6:6–7). He reverts to the same powerful image in an autobiographical account inserted in one of his pamphlets of 1642. Here he shows the poet as a vessel of the "eternall Spirit, who can enrich with all utterance and knowledge, and sends out his Seraphim with the hallow'd fire of his Altar to touch and purify the lips of whom he pleases."[7]

To Charles Diodati above all he felt able to open his mind concerning his aspirations. In September 1637 he wrote to his friend, giving the time consumed by study as the reason for his slowness as a correspondent. His disposition is such, he declares, "that no delay, no rest, no thought or care for anything else can divert me from my purpose until I reach my goal and complete some great cycle of my studies."[8] A second letter several weeks later conveyed a fuller revelation of himself:

> ...though I know not God's intent for me in other respects, yet of this I am sure, that he has imbued me especially with a mighty passion for Beauty. Ceres never her sought her daughter Proserpine (as the legend tells) with greater ardor than I do this Idea of Beauty, like some image of loveliness; ever pursuing it, by day and by night, in every shape and form...and following close in its footprints as it leads.

"You ask, What am I thinking about," he continues:

---

[7] *The Reason of Church-Government Urg'd against Prelaty*, 1642, CPW, vol. I, p. 821.

[8] E. M. W. Tillyard and P. B. Tillyard, *Milton. Private Correspondence And Academic Exercises* (Cambridge: Cambridge University Press, 1932), p. 11.

So help me God, of immortality. What am I doing? Growing wings
and learning to fly; but my Pegasus can only rise on tender pinions as
yet, so let my new wisdom be humble.[9]

In the last and finest of his university exercises Milton expressed
his many sided conception of learning and the blessings it bestows.
"...nothing common or mediocre," he said, could be tolerated in a
poet or orator, and both must possess a thorough knowledge of the
arts and sciences for their calling.[10] Later on, the notes on his reading
in his *Commonplace Book* demonstrate the wide extent and methodical
character of his private studies. Ancient, medieval, and ecclesiastical
history in the west and east; the history of Italy and the Italian cities,
of the Reformation, England, Scotland, Ireland, France, and Russia;
Greek, Roman, and modern literature; the church fathers; the history
of political theory; mathematics and music; all fell within his scope.[11]
The composition of a great epic poem on British history also
increasingly occupied his mind, and he jotted down a list of more
than thirty subjects as possible themes.[12] A Latin poem he wrote in
Italy in praise of the Neapolitan nobleman Manso, who had shown
him great consideration, voiced his hope of recalling to life in song
the kings of his native land and Arthur and the great-hearted heroes
of the Round Table. (*Mansus*, 80–82).

But if his mind was filled with exalted thoughts of the poet's role
and his project of a great work, he was also sometimes troubled by a
sense of tardiness in the fulfillment of his gifts. In his *Seventh Sonnet*
commemorating his twenty-third year, he laments his swiftly
passing youth and continued immaturity:

> My hasting days fly on with full career,
> But my late spring no bird or blossom sheweth.
> Perhaps my semblance might deceive the truth,
> That I to manhood am arrived so near,
> And inward ripeness doth much less appear
> That some more timely-happy spirits endueth.

The poem ends, however, with the calm assurance that he will put his
gifts to use if he patiently pursues his course in obedience to God's
will.

---

[9] Ibid., p. 14.
[10] *The Seventh Prolusion in Defence of Learning*, 1632?, CPW, vol. I, pp. 287–288.
[11] Milton's *Commonplace Book* is printed in CPW, vol. I; see the editor's
introduction, p. 348.
[12] Parker, vol. I, pp. 190–192.

The same deliberate aim of preparation stands out in a letter he addressed to an unnamed friend enclosing this sonnet, which also touches revealingly on the subject of his "tardie moving." The friend, who may have been been his much respected former tutor, Thomas Young, a Scottish Puritan minister, had reproved him for his too great love of learning and of dreaming his life away in studious retirement instead of entering the ministry. In reply, Milton acknowledged that he felt the true scholar's desire for honor and immortal fame which ought to dissuade him from prolonged obscurity. Nevertheless, he justified the necessity of his lengthy pursuit of learning in order to fit him better to employ his talent as God wished. He would therefore take "no thought of beeing late so it gave advantage to be more fit...."[13]

His father too was dissatisfied with his postponement of a career and had also criticized his dedication to poetry, as is apparent from a Latin poem written about 1634 that Milton addressed to him. Although affectionate and respectful, his response to his father's view reaffirms his dedication to his art and is infused with the idealistic conception of the poet and a belief in his own future greatness. He expressed his deep gratitude for his father's generosity, which he could never repay. He likewise begged him not to despise "divine poetry" or scorn the "sacred Muses" as worthless or unprofitable; nor could he believe, he said, that his father really hated the Muses, since his musical ability derived from them. He reminded the elder Milton, moreover, that he had not forced his son to strive for wealth, but allowed him leisure to cultivate his mind with all knowledge. The conclusion voiced his hope of attaining immortality by his poems together with the promise that his eulogy and his father's name would thereby be preserved to far off ages. (*Ad Patrem*).[14]

Of Milton's early work, *Lycidas*, a pastoral elegy written in 1637,

[13] CPW, vol. I, pp. 319–321; this undated letter was probably written in 1632 or 1633.

[14] The undated *Ad Patrem* has been variously assigned to 1632, 1634, 1637, and several later years; see the discussion in CF, p. 148. Parker, vol. II, p. 788 n.25, argues persuasively that it was written in 1634. I cannot, however, agree with his view (vol. I, pp. 125–126) that Milton treats poetry in it as merely a pleasant vocation and an amusement and pastime which he asks his father not to condemn. If *Ad Patrem* clearly implies a crisis in his relationship with his father, as Parker believes, then it was surely not because Milton considered poetry a pastime. The poem's image of the poet and poetry is highly idealistic. It is also noteworthy that Milton says nothing to reassure his father about his pursuit of a career. Tillyard rightly comments on the "consummate firmness" with which Milton in this poem put his father in his place; E. M. W. Tillyard, *Milton*, 4th impression (London: Chatto and Windus, 1949), p. 78.

contains his most poignant reflections on fame and immortality. It was composed to honor the memory of Edward King, represented in the poem as the deceased shepherd Lycidas, a Fellow of Christ's College and friend or acquaintance of Milton who had recently drowned in a shipwreck in the Irish Sea. The elegy's narrative voice is that of a bereaved shepherd who with deep feeling mourns and praises the young Lycidas, "dead ere his prime." It was inevitable that King's fate should have caused Milton to confront the uncertainty of his own personal future; for like Milton, King, who was four years younger, was also destined for the ministry and a poet who knew how "to sing, and build the lofty rhyme." The fundamental question the poem raises concerns the working of divine justice in the world and whether there is any point to the arduous effort and disciplined dedication required for a high calling if death can prematurely cut one off, as it had Lycidas. Would it not be preferable simply to enjoy life's sensual pleasures and

> To sport with Amaryllis in the shade
> Or with the tangles of Neaera's hair,

as others do? (67–69)

As an explanation for such dedication the lamenting shepherd points to the pursuit of fame:

> Fame is the spur that the clear spirit doth raise
> (That last infirmity of noble mind)
> To scorn delights and live laborious days.   (70–72)

But not only is the thirst for fame admitted here to be a weakness, but the shepherd immediately reflects that death may prevent its attainment:

> But the fair guerdon when we hope to find,
> And think to burst out into sudden blaze,
> Comes the blind Fury with th'abhorred shears,
> And slits the thin-spun life.   (73–76)

The ensuing solace arises from the realization, imparted to the shepherd by Apollo, that true fame does not grow on mortal soil or consist in worldly report. It lies rather in the sight of God, "all-judging Jove," who grants fame in heaven as a reward in accordance with one's deeds. (78–84)

At the elegy's conclusion the shepherd arrives at the ultimate consolation. He bids the other grieving shepherds to weep no more, for "sunk though he be beneath the watery floor," Lycidas is not dead, but through Christ's power has been raised to heaven,

...the blest kingdoms meek of joy and love.
There entertain him all the saints above,
In solemn troops and sweet societies
That sing, and singing in their glory move
And wipe the tears forever from his eyes.   (177–182)

The final lines imply the lyric speaker's resolution of doubt and the
restoration of his spiritual equilibrium in the face of life's
uncertainties:

And now the sun had stretched out all the hills,
And now was dropped into the western bay;
At last he rose and twitched his mantle blue:
Tomorrow to fresh woods and pastures new.   (190–194)

I don't think it is the case, as Tillyard has suggested, that Edward
King is only the nominal subject of *Lycidas*, whose real subject is
Milton himself.[15] Milton has taken care to observe the decorum
required of the elegiac form in which he is writing by not intruding
his own personality into the work. It is impossible to read it,
nonetheless, without seeing in it a pattern resembling his own
experience. The longing for fame and belief in his destiny were
central to his identity, yet he had also been made vividly aware of the
possibility of early death before he could reach his goal. *Lycidas* in its
progression of moods seems to represent a reconciliation of these
feelings. He does not renounce the idea of fame, but sublimates it in
the recognition that immortality comes as the reward of doing those
things worthy of God's approval. He does not regard the future
fearfully, but turns toward it with confidence as a poet who in his
deeds keeps in mind "all-judging Jove."

About the time he wrote *Lycidas*, Milton may have conclusively
decided against becoming a minister. The exact date of this decision
remains uncertain. Five years later, however, in a pamphlet attacking
episcopacy, he recorded that after attaining "some maturity of
yeers," he perceived that "tyranny had invaded the church" and that
his conscience had refused to "subscribe slave" by swearing the oath
and articles required for taking orders. The anger of this passage, in
which Milton also complains that he was "Church-outed by the

---

15 Tillyard, pp. 80–91. Tillyard holds that *Lycidas* is one of Milton's most personal
poems, but it needn't follow from this fact that he was its real subject; see M. H.
Abrams' discussion of this and other interpretations in "Five Types of *Lycidas*,"
Doing Things with Texts. Essays in Criticism And Critical Theory (New York: Norton,
1989).

Prelats,"[16] has its counterpart in *Lycidas*. In the latter the shepherd depicts the apostle Peter, "the pilot of the Galilean lake," lamenting the loss of Lycidas, for whose presence he would gladly spare the ignorant men who assume the pastoral office solely "for their bellies' sake." These have no other care than

> ...how to scramble at the shearers' feast,
> And shove away the worthy bidden guest;
> Blind mouths! that scarce themselves know how to hold
> A sheep-hook, or have learned aught else the least
> That to the faithful herdsman's art belongs.   (117–121)

These and the succeeding lines, which express bitter condemnation of a corrupt clergy incapable of preaching and neglectful of their flocks, perhaps indicate that Milton had by now become so alienated from the established church that he no longer wished to enter its ministry.

One of the most striking aspects of Milton's self-formation is the high importance he attributed to chastity in his early writings. Although the necessity of a virtuous life was basic to his conception of the poet, within that view chastity assumed unusual prominence in the preparation he believed he must undergo as one set apart for the attainment of great things. This did not mean, though, that he was indifferent to sex or unattracted to women; indeed the contrary was certainly the case.[17] In his *Fifth Elegy*, a joyous celebration of the advent of spring written when he was twenty, the images are rich in sensual appeal and sexual overtones. The lascivious earth, eager for the embraces of Phoebus, voluptuously bares her breasts, breathing mild perfume and roses from her lovely lips, while the girls, their virgin breasts bound about with gold, greet the spring with a prayer to Venus to grant them the man of their desire. (55–60, 95, 109–113). In an earlier poem, he tells of girl-watching in London and how he was often struck dumb by the shapeliness of a girl's figure, by her eyes brighter than jewels or stars, her enticing cheeks and neck, and "that flowing way...drenched in pure nectarous milk." (*First Elegy*, 51–58). The *Seventh Elegy* reports that a glance from a beautiful girl

---

[16] *The Reason of Church-Government*, pp. 822–823. The oath which Milton said he was unwilling to subscribe could have been the so-called Etcetera Oath imposed on the clergy by the canons passed in the spring of 1640 while Archbishop Laud still retained his dominance over the church. If this were the case, then it is possible that Milton may not have finally decided against entering the ministry until shortly after that date.

[17] See Edward Le Comte, *Milton And Sex* (London: Macmillan, 1978), chap. 1.

had smitten him with love and that now, his being aflame, he remains Cupid's hapless victim, plunged in a misery which is yet somehow delightful. (61–77, 95–100).

Despite the susceptibility to desire and intense physical response to feminine beauty manifest in many passages of his early work,[18] the youthful Milton's sense of vocation caused him to subject his sexuality to strict control. In the *Sixth Elegy*, for example, he stressed that the poet, whom he likened to a priest, must be chaste in youth and frugal in his life. (60–63). Several years later, in his letter to the unnamed friend with whom he discussed his delay of a career, he stated that for the sake of his self-preparation he was willing to forego or postpone his natural inclination to marriage and a family.[19] Most of all in *Comus*, the masque presented in 1634 at Ludlow Castle, chastity is praised. The drama of its plot arises from the conflict between sensuality and the naturalistic affirmation of unfettered sexuality personified by the lascivious spirit Comus, and the principle of temperance, self-discipline, and chastity personified by the Lady. Although lost in a wood and separated from her two brothers, the Lady is guarded by Faith, Hope, and the "Unblemished form of chastity." (212–214). In their fears for her safety, the Elder Brother reassures the Younger that she possesses a hidden strength given her by heaven:

> 'Tis chastity, my brother, chastity:
> She that has that, is clad in complete steel,
> ....   (419–420)
> ....
> So dear to heaven is saintly chastity
> That when a soul is found sincerely so,
> A thousand liveried angels lackey her,
> Driving far off each thing of sin and guilt,
> ...   (452–455)

After her abduction by Comus disguised as a shepherd, the Lady haughtily repels his advances and overawes him by the power of her virtue. Invoking the doctrine of chastity against his clever arguments in favor of sexual freedom, she contemptuously tells him:

---

[18] Although the amatory passages in his early writings, with their extensive mythological references, were heavily indebted to the conventions of classical erotic verse (Ovid was one of Milton's favorite poets and models), their reality of feeling and delight in their theme are unmistakable; see the comments in J. H. Hanford's seminal essay, "The Youth of Milton," (first published in 1925), *John Milton Poet And Humanist* (Cleveland: Western Reserve University Press, 1966), pp. 26–27.

[19] CPW, vol. I, p. 319.

Thou hast nor ear, nor soul to apprehend
The sublime notion and high mystery
That must be uttered to unfold the sage
And serious doctrine of virginity,
... (783–786)

In the end, with the help of an Attendant Spirit and the Nymph Sabrina, Comus and his riotous crew are routed and the Lady, freed and reunited with her brothers, returns safely with them to their parents at Ludlow Castle.

Comus was surely extraordinary in substituting chastity for charity in the famous trinity of virtues listed by St Paul in his letter to the Corinthians (1 Corinthians 13:13).[20] This was not a Protestant belief. While Protestantism taught the necessity of abstinence before marriage and restraint and marital fidelity thereafter, it did not elevate chastity into a supreme virtue. Why did Milton embrace it as an ethical ideal? I believe he did so because he saw in it not only a sign of purity but an enhancement of the self-mastery and inner concentration of spiritual forces on which he was intent. Possibly he even believed at the time that chastity could endow him with magical power in his growth as a poet.[21]

The fullest account of his attitude in the matter appears in an autobiographical segment of one of his anti-prelatical tracts published in 1642 to answer a personal attack by a defender of episcopacy. His opponent had impugned his character and accused him of frequenting bordellos. In self-vindication Milton told his readers how at an early age he was confirmed in the opinion that one who wished to write well of laudable things

> ought him selfe to bee a true Poem, that is, a composition of, and patterne of the best and honourablest things, not presuming to sing high praises of heroick men, or famous Cities, unlesse he have in himself the experience and the practice of all that which is praise-worthy.

Subsequently, he continued, his younger feet led him to the fables and romances recounting the deeds of knighthood and victorious British kings, whence he learned "what a noble vertue chastity must be, to the defence of which so many worthies by such a deare adventure of themselves had sworne." Then in riper years his

---

[20] See CF, pp. 172–173, for a review of the scholarly comments on the role of chastity in *Comus*.

[21] See Tillyard's discussion, pp. 73, 74–75, and Appendix C, "The Doctrine of Chastity in Milton."

ceaseless round of study brought him to philosophy and Plato's divine volumes, which taught him the nature of chastity and true love, "whose charming cup is only vertue which she bears in her hand to those who are worthy." The scriptures too had unfolded to him the "chaste and high mysteries" in St Paul's injunction that "the body is for the Lord and the Lord for the body." (1 Corinthians 6:13). By this saying he was made to understand that if unchastity was a scandal and dishonor to a woman, it was much more so to a man, who is both the image and glory of God and the more perfect sex. Alluding to Revelation 14:1–5, he also noted the effect upon him of the place in Scripture expressing the

> high rewards ever accompanying the Lambe, with those celestial songs to others inapprehensible, but not to those who were not defil'd with women, which doubtlesse meanes fornication: For mariage must not be call'd a defilement.[22]

These statements provide a remarkable commentary on the influence the idea of chastity exerted over Milton's mind in the course of his formative years. Its main sources lay in the Platonic doctrine of the soul's ascent from its sensual trammels to a spiritual vision of love and truth, reinforced by the scriptural teaching of St Paul. It may well be that in the passage from the Book of Revelation about the celestial songs accompanying the Lamb, he also discerned a special meaning applicable to himself as a singer of these songs. His denial that marriage falls under the ban against defilement with women is significant in this context. In spite of the Lady's praise in *Comus* of "the sage and serious doctrine of virginity," it is doubtful that he ever considered marriage to be a defilement, and he would have been far indeed from the Protestant understanding of marriage if he had done so. But his insistence on the point at this time may indicate that by then he had reversed his earlier intention not to marry. This might be concluded from the fact that the pamphlet in which it appeared was published in April 1642, only a few short weeks before his precipitous marriage to Mary Powell.[23]

Milton did not hide his light under a bushel, and among the five anti–episcopal pamphlets he wrote in 1641–42 he allowed himself to include some extraordinarily personal revelations. We might wonder why he joined in the controversy over episcopacy which broke out with the assembling of the Long Parliament in November 1640.

---

[22] *An Apology against A Pamphlet*, pp. 890–892.
[23] For the *Apology*'s date, see the editor's remarks, ibid., p. 862.

Despite his wide learning and desire for reformation, he had no special qualifications or experience for dealing with the vexed problem of church government. In 1654, in an autobiographical account in his *Second Defence of The English People*, he explained that he did so because he believed that if he wished to be of use in the future, he must not fail his country or fellow Christians at a time of so much danger.[24] In 1641–42, his statements leave no doubt that he entered the controversy not only for religious and patriotic reasons, but impelled by the same prophetic sense of his own chosenness that he felt as a poet. The fourth of his anti-episcopal tracts contained an elaborate apology for his involvement denying that vainglory or other unworthy motives had incited him to contend in print with men of high estimation, especially as he had not yet completed the full circle of his private studies. He noted, moreover, that the power of nature led him to another task than writing in the "cool element" of prose, in which he had, as it were, only the use of his left hand. Nevertheless, he considered himself as divinely summoned, and recalling the prophet Jeremiah, declared that "when God commands to take the trumpet and blow a dolorous or jarring blast, it lies not in mans will what he shall say, or what he shall conceal." Ease and leisure had been given him for his retired thoughts "out of the sweat of other men," and now God listened for his voice among the faithful servants who rose to the defense of religion when its cause was at stake.[25]

Not content with this apology, he went on to relate considerably more about himself. These remarks were a pure digression, irrelevant to the issues he was addressing. It was naive, moreover, and suggestive of a sublime egotism for him to assume that his contemporaries, to whom he was hardly known, would feel the extent of interest in him that his statements imply.

What followed was a highly personal narrative offering a striking portrayal of the author's self-formation and his overwhelming ambition as a poet-prophet.[26] Telling first of his careful education, he

[24] *Second Defence*, p. 622.

[25] *The Reason of Church-Government*, pp. 803, 804–805, 806–808.

[26] First published in 1927, H. J. C. Grierson, *Milton & Wordsworth Poets And Prophets. A Study of Their Relation to Political Events*, 4th impression (London: Chatto and Windus, 1960), remains a penetrating discussion of Milton's belief in his prophetic vocation. William Kerrigan, *The Prophetic Milton* (Charlottesville: University Press of Virginia, 1974), and John Spencer Hill, *John Milton: Poet, Priest And Prophet. A Study of Divine Vocation in Milton's Poetry And Prose* (London: Macmillan, 1979), contain fuller treatments of the same subject, including material on the biblical, classical, and Protestant background to the concept of prophetic vocation.

reports how his teachers found that whatever he wrote, whether in English or a foreign tongue or in prose or verse, but especially the latter, "the stile by certain vital signes it had, was likely to live." Later, the encomia he won in Italy by his poetry convinced him that

> by labour and intent study (which I take to be my portion in this life) joyn'd with the strong propensity of nature, I might perhaps leave something so written to aftertimes. as they should not willingly let it die.

For the honor and instruction of his country, he said that he chose to attempt this task in the English language. He wished to be an interpreter of the best and wisest things to his fellow-citizens, and what the greatest and choicest minds of Athens, Rome, modern Italy, and the ancient Hebrews did for their country, this he hoped to do for his own. He ascribed the highest value to the poet's abilities as the inspired gift of God, bestowed on but a few in every nation, and possessing the power

> to imbreed and cherish in a great people the seeds of vertu, and publick civility, to allay the perturbation of the mind, and set the affections in right tune, to celebrate in glorious and lofty Hymns the throne and equipage of Gods Almightinesse, and what he works, and what he suffers to be wrought with high providence in his Church, to sing the victorious agonies of Martyrs and Saints, the deeds and triumphs of just and pious nations...to deplore the general relapse of Kingdoms and States from justice and Gods true Worship.

In conclusion, he asked the knowing reader to trust him for a few years yet, promising that with God's inspiration, and granted time for further study and observation, he would make good on his intention to produce the great work he had in mind.[27]

The idealistic self-confidence Milton displays in this account would be hard to exceed. It is paralleled by a passage in another of these tracts in which, in an eloquent prayer of thanksgiving to God for leading his country to a great reformation, he refers indirectly to himself and his plan for a great epic poem:

> Then amidst the Hymns and Halleluiahs of Saints, some one may perhaps bee heard offering at high strains in new and lofty Measures to sing and celebrate thy divine Mercies, and marvelous Judgements in this Land throughout all Ages; whereby this great and Warlike Nation, instructed and iniur'd to the fervent and continuall practice of

---

[27] *The Reason of Church Government*, pp. 809–810,812, 813, 816–817, 821–822.

17

Truth and Righteousnesse...may presse on hard to that high and happy Emulation to be found the soberest, wisest, and most Christian People....

And he goes on to imply that at the day of Christ's coming, he will be among those who shall receive "above the inferiour Orders of the Blessed" additional honors because of their services to the common good of religion and their country.[28]

I have already quoted several statements about his development from the last of Milton's anti-prelatical tracts, *An Apology Against A Pamphlet*.[29] Compelled in self-defense, he said, to enter into his own praises, here as well he refers to the gifts imparted to him by God, "which I boast not but thankfully acknowledge...." Again he intimates his expectation of future greatness in describing how his youthful study of the glorious achievement of the great orators, historians, and poets of the past made him believe "by every instinct and presage of nature which is not wont to be false, that what imbolden'd them to this task might with such diligence as they used imbolden me...." In an affirmation of his commitment to the exemplary conduct befitting a poet aspiring to the highest ends, he asserts that "together with a certain nicenesse of nature, an honest haughtinesse, and self-esteem either of what I was, or what I might be, (which let envie call pride)," had always kept him from doing anything beneath himself.[30]

Milton penned these words at the age of thirty-three. Like his other statements about himself, they attest to the deliberate sense of purpose and hope of immortal fame that shaped his youth. In every atom of his being he felt himself to be born an aristocrat of the mind and spirit. He considered the talent he possessed by nature as likewise the gift of grace to him from God. Although he had still not produced the great work he promised, he was confident that he would do so. The conviction of his difference and superiority to others as a man marked out for the performance of something great colored his entire personality. This same consciousness, as we shall see, also largely determined his political view of the world in the permutations it would undergo during the course of the English revolution.

---

[28] *Of Reformation Touching Church-Discipline*, 1641, CPW, vol. I, p. 616.

[29] *An Apology against A Pamphlet* was Milton's reply to an attack on himself in another pamphlet whose authors were probably the bishop of Norwich, Joseph Hall, and his son John Hall; see the editor's introduction to *An Apology*, CPW, vol. I, pp. 862–863.

[30] *Ibid.*, pp. 869, 883, 889, 890.

What, however, were Milton's political beliefs and social values during the years of his self-formation? These were also the years of increasing conflict between the Court and the Country, which was to culminate after 1640 in a revolution against the Stuart monarchy.[31] Shortly after Milton entered Cambridge in 1625, Charles I succeeded his father James I on the throne. The first part of the new king's reign, which saw the meeting of three separate parliaments between 1625 and 1628, revealed the growing differences dividing the crown from the greater part of the governing class whose members dominated the kingdom's great representative assembly. At the time England was carrying on wars with both France and Spain, wars that lasted until 1630 and were widely unpopular because of the many burdens they imposed and the government's military failures. When the parliament of 1626 refused the king's request for financial assistance to sustain his military efforts, he resorted to forced loans, imprisonment of refusers, and other measures which provoked widespread political opposition and charges of illegality and arbitrary government. In 1628 the king's third parliament pressured him into assenting to the Petition of Right, a reaffirmation of ancient liberties and statutes intended to restrain the royal prerogative within lawful limits. In its second session of 1629, however, bitter distrust and dissension over religious and political questions led to a breakdown in the relations between the king and parliament. Concluding that it was unmanageable, Charles I resolved to govern in the future without consulting parliament, which did not meet again for the next eleven years. At the same time royal religious policy incited the opposition of Puritans and moderate Protestants, as the king showed himself averse to the Calvinistic theology that had hitherto been the foundation of the Anglican church. He placed the administration of the church in the hands of Arminian clergy headed by William Laud, bishop of London, who in 1633 was appointed archbishop of

---

[31] The origins of the English revolution are a highly controversial subject that has provoked an extensive debate. The accounts given in my *The Court And The Country* (New York: Atheneum, 1970), and in Lawrence Stone's *The Causes of The English Revolution 1529–1642* (London: Routledge & Kegan Paul, 1972), have been challenged by numerous revisionist scholars, most notably Conrad Russell, who has set forth his own explanation of events in three successive works, *Parliament And English Politics 1621–1629* (Oxford: Oxford University Press, 1979); *The Causes of The English Civil War* (Oxford: Oxford University Press, 1990), and *The Fall of The British Monarchy* (Oxford: Oxford University Press, 1991). R. C. Richardson, *The Debate on The English Revolution Revisited* (London: Routledge & Kegan Paul, 1988), has surveyed the literature of this controversy. The introduction and essays in *Conflict in Early Stuart England*, ed. Richard Cust and Ann Hughes (London: Longman, 1989), deal with what they call its post-revisionist phase.

Canterbury. These churchmen rejected the doctrine of predestination, which most religious people regarded as the core of Protestantism, introduced ritualistic innovations that critics denounced as the entering wedge of popery, and persecuted Puritans who resisted these changes.[32] Toward the close of the 1630s the conditions making for revolution ripened. In Scotland the royal attempt to introduce alterations in religion in line with those in England provoked the outbreak of rebellion in 1638 which proclaimed the Scottish National Covenant as its symbol. In England, the ship money tax, an exaction imposed on the country at the king's sole will, convinced the government's opponents that it was bent on absolutism without regard for the liberty or property of subjects. In the spring of 1640, desperate to obtain money and aid to suppress the rebellion in Scotland, Charles I decided after a long intermission to seek the help of parliament once more. It proved so hostile and uncooperative that he dissolved it after only three weeks. Following this failure, the army of the Scottish Covenanters invaded and occupied the counties of northern England. The Scottish revolt fostered further disaffection in England, and the regime was plunged into crisis, its power paralyzed in the face of its English subjects increasing disobedience and defiance of its commands. Lacking any alternative and helpless in the face of a general demand throughout the kingdom, the king in the autumn of 1640 was finally compelled to call another parliament to deal with the crisis. The assembling on 3 November of what was to become known as the Long Parliament marked the beginning of a revolution, though none could then foresee how far it would carry the nation from its old landmarks.

Milton lived through all these developments and would have been aware of them in a general way. Nevertheless, his writings of the 1630s contain little indication of a concern with current politics. The principal overt expression suggesting such an interest appeared in *Lycidas*'s denunciation of clerical corruption, which has been mentioned earlier. Through the mouth of the apostle Peter the poet pronounced a stern indictment of greedy, mercenary pastors heedless of the spiritual welfare of their flocks, predicting their destruction by "that two-handed engine at the door" which "stands ready to smite once, and smite no more." (130–131). The passage should perhaps be related to Milton's friendship with the Scottish Puritan Thomas Young, his former tutor. In 1637, at the time he wrote *Lycidas*, Young, a man of presbyterian leanings critical of the established

32 See Nicholas Tyacke, *Anti-Calvinists. The Rise of English Arminianism c. 1590–1640* (Oxford: Clarendon Press, 1989).

church, held a clerical living at Stowmarket in Suffolk, and Milton's friendship and respect for him would likely have influenced his own feeling about the church.[33] Another of his friends, Alexander Gill junior, the son of the headmaster of St Paul's school with whom he exchanged Latin verses, got into serious trouble in 1628 for his statements attacking the duke of Buckingham, Charles I's favorite and chief minister. He was sentenced to a heavy punishment, including degradation from the ministry and loss of his ears, but was finally pardoned and succeeded his father in 1635 as head of St Paul's. Milton's friendship with Gill may also have affected his political attitudes.[34]

Too much significance should not be ascribed to these associations, however, for Milton may not have paid a great deal of attention to public affairs through most of the 1630s. The strained attempt of Marxist critics to discover a radical political meaning in his earlier work must be dismissed as pure wish projection.[35] Nor have we any reason to believe that censorship may have prevented him from expressing his true opinions. In 1638, the date of *Lycidas*'s publication as part of a memorial volume to Edward King by his Cambridge friends, government censorship of Puritan propaganda was at its height. In the previous year the Court of Star Chamber inflicted a severe punishment on the Puritans Bastwick, Burton, and Prynne to make an example of them for their libels against the bishops. The court also issued an important decree tightening control of the press in order to stop unlicensed printing.[36] Thus if, as is not unlikely, Milton intended his invective in *Lycidas* to apply to the church under Archbishop Laud, then censorship did not inhibit him from publishing these highly critical statements. There is no evidence to warrant the notion that his verse of this period needs decoding or was driven to disguise or indirection by his fear of censorship.[37]

[33] For Thomas Young and his Puritanism, see *D. N. B.*, s.v.

[34] On Alexander Gill the younger, see *D. N. B.*, s.v.

[35] See Michael Wilding, *Dragon's Teeth. Literature in the English Revolution* (Oxford: Clarendon Press, 1987), chaps. 2–3, and David Norbrook, *Poetry And Politics In The English Renaissance* (London: Routledge & Kegan Paul, 1984), chap. 10, for examples of such coercive interpretations in behalf of a radical reading of Milton's earlier work.

[36] S. R. Gardiner, *History of England from The Accession of James I to The Outbreak of The Civil War*, 10 vols. (London, 1884), vol. VIII, pp. 228–229, 234–235.

[37] For the view that Milton was deterred by censorship, see Christopher Hill, *Milton And The English Revolution* (London: Faber and Faber, 1977), pp. 50–52. Equally unlikely is the implication (p. 52) that Milton concealed his authorship of *Lycidas* by signing it only with his initials when it was first published in 1638, a device that could not have prevented any hostile inquirer from establishing his

Despite the general agreement that Milton was a Puritan, it is hard to know exactly what his Puritanism consisted of at this time, especially as until 1641 his writings contain no direct comments on religious controversies. Nothing in his personal history indicates that he ever underwent the agonizing wrestling with conscience or the experience of conversion such as many Puritans knew in their lives during their passage from oppression by sin to the assurance of grace and election. Nor does he ever speak of the central Calvinist principle of double predestination which Puritans along with many other English Protestants accepted as orthodox doctrine and which they condemned the Arminian clergy for disavowing. Although Milton was later to abandon this belief himself, whether he ever questioned it in the 1630s is unknown. The main signs of his Puritan orientation appear to have lain in the strictness of the moral principles by which he tried to govern himself, as well as in his conviction of election and God's guidance and the dedication of his poetic gift to God's service. Along with these beliefs, he also shared the keen hostility to Catholicism as a false and tyrannous religion which Puritans were apt to feel. We can hardly doubt, moreover, that he felt a strong antipathy to the Laudian ceremonial innovations and repression in the Anglican church.

A number of the entries in Milton's *Commonplace Book* cover political topics noted from his reading under headings such as "The State," "King," "Subject," "The King of England," "Property And Taxes," "Of Sedition," and "Tyrant." Most of these, however, belong to the 1640s or later, according to the editor's dating. Several, conjecturally assigned to 1639–41, refer to Magna Carta and the liberties of subjects and of parliament; others of the same presumed date note the danger of a royal marriage to a spouse of another religion, an allusion to Charles I's marriage to a Catholic wife, and condemn the use of law French in statutes as "norman gibberish." While the *Commonplace Book* cites some of the works and authors that were among the sources of Milton's later republicanism and belief in

identity. Michael Wilding and Joseph Wittreich are among the recent Milton scholars who have echoed Hill's opinion that Milton was concerned about the problem of censorship in his earlier work, while Annabel Patterson has discussed the strategies by which seventeenth-century writers attempted to evade the censor; Wilding, pp. 21, 27, 29; Joseph Wittreich, *Feminist Milton* (Ithaca: Cornell University Press, 1987), p. 28; Annabel Patterson, *Censorship And Interpretation: The Condition of Reading And Writing in Early Modern England* (Madison: University of Wisconsin Press, 1984). In spite of these claims in regard to Milton, no scholar has produced any evidence that he felt threatened by censorship before the civil war or modified his expression because of it.

popular sovereignty, his notes provide little information either about his actual political views or the extent of his political interests before the Long Parliament.[38]

To understand Milton not only at this period but during the earlier stages of the English revolution, it is necessary to keep in mind how academic and remote his knowledge of life still was. Save for his fifteen-month journey across France to Italy, he had spent all his time in study. He had never been compelled to earn his livelihood or enter a profession. After returning from his European tour he took a house in the autumn of 1640 in the city of London on Aldersgate Street where he kept a school for a handful of pupils. Thus far he had known but few adversities. Probably the worst blows he had suffered were his mother's death in 1637 and the unexpected death the following year of Charles Diodati, whose tragic loss he commemorated in *Epitaphium Damonis*, an elegy for his dearest friend. Although acquainted with some of his father's business dealings in lending money and placing mortgages, he had little practical contact with affairs and had never held any public responsibilities. Dedicated to becoming a great poet and scholar, he saw the world largely through the medium of books. A Puritan humanist nourished on the scriptures and the myths and literature of Greco-Roman antiquity, he was dominated by his sense of vocation and deeply idealistic in his personal goals and general outlook. He had no understanding of the realities of politics, and all his political conceptions were still founded on abstractions and heavily influenced by his classical reading. In his basic standpoint he remained a thorough intellectual concerned above all with morality, and it was largely from a moral standpoint that he approached the world of politics.

Aside from *Lycidas*, the works among his earlier poetry that offer the fullest insight into his political and social values are *Arcades* and *Comus*. Both are entertainments in a courtly mode, celebrations of aristocracy designed for performance, as the heading of *Arcades* states, "by noble persons," and both reflect the author's accord with the hierarchic society of his age based on the dominance of a landed aristocratic order and on the principles of birth, status, honor, deference, and subordination. Born into the middle rank of this society himself and of a father whose affiliation with commerce and

---

[38] *Commonplace Book*, pp. 399, 424, 446–447, 449. Milton's notes contain some other entries on political topics which the editor also assigns to 1639–41, but the dating in all these cases is uncertain, and they could as easily belong to a later as to an earlier date.

money lending might conceivably have even debarred the latter from being regarded as a gentleman, Milton's attitude to this noble order observes the conventions of deference.[39] At the same time, though, he places before it, particularly in *Comus*, the ideal moral standards he deems essential to a political and social elite.

Arcades, which was written about 1633, consists of verses to honor the countess dowager of Derby at a family celebration held for her at Harefield, her Middlesex estate. Then over seventy, she was also through a later marriage the widow of Sir Thomas Egerton, Viscount Brackley, Lord Chancellor of England, and she and her husband had once entertained Queen Elizabeth at Harefield. The arrangement for Milton to write a work for the occasion was doubtless due to Henry Lawes, a friend of Milton's father and a connection of the Egerton family, to whose children he had taught music. Lawes was a noted musician and composer, a member of the King's Music who played a role in the artistic life of the Caroline court, and he also provided the music for Milton's words. The poem presents some of the countess's family as Arcadians who are guided to her presence by the Genius of The Wood. The latter praises her wisdom, worth, and majesty,

> Sitting like a goddess bright
> In the centre of her light. (18–19)

He speaks of the Sirens' celestial music which only the pure can hear:

> And yet such music worthiest were to blaze
> The peerless height of her immortal praise,
> Whose lustre leads us, and for her most fit,
> If my inferior hand or voice could hit
> Inimitable sounds....

Promising to attend the nymphs and shepherds

> toward her glittering state;
> Where ye may all that are of noble stem
> Approach, and kiss her sacred vesture's hem. (81–83),

he leads them to her and hails her as

[39] Milton's father displayed a coat of arms bearing a spread eagle with two heads apparently based on the arms of the Scriveners Company; Parker, vol. II, p. 689. Although he was a respected business man who had held offices in the company, the aristocratic standards prevailing in the earlier seventeenth century relegated men engaged in trade to the citizen and urban order of society and did not acknowledge them as gentlemen. Milton himself could claim to be a gentleman in virtue of being a university graduate. His seal also bore a spread eagle with two heads as his arms; ibid., vol. II, p. 1097.

Such a rural queen
All Arcadia hath not seen. (94–95).

We must imagine this scene being performed in the park or garden at Harefield by the younger members of the countess's family as they troop in their Arcadian costumes to pay her the homage proclaimed in Milton's lines. *Arcades* is both a tribute to nobility and a perfect compliment to an aristocratic matriarch whom it depicts as a regal personage. While it idealizes themes of deference, kinship, and obligation basic to the aristocratic way of life, it also presupposes a conception of true nobility as residing principally in virtue, here harmoniously blended with the hereditary principle.[40]

In *Comus*, a much longer, more complex work, the moral quality of nobility is given a far richer treatment. First titled *A Masque Presented at Ludlow Castle*, *Comus* is a pastoral allegory belonging to the genre of dramatic entertainment most favored by the Stuart court, in which not only courtiers but Queen Henrietta Maria and Charles I himself sometimes took part. Court masques were lavish theatrical spectacles, glorifications of love and kingship containing neo-Platonic themes and created by the foremost poets, designers, and musicians of the day. As one of its leading students has characterized it, the masque form presented the triumph of an aristocratic community and had at its center a belief in hierarchy and a faith in the power of idealization. Although scholars have been at pains to point out the ways in which *Comus* differed from other masques of the period, Milton's work, despite these differences, nevertheless conforms generally to this description and should be seen in both its nature and appeal as essentially a species of aristocratic art.[41]

[40] See the discussion in Cedric M. Brown, *John Milton's Aristocratic Entertainments* (Cambridge: Cambridge University Press), chap. 2, esp. pp. 46–47.
[41] Stephen Orgel, *The Illusion of Power* (Berkeley: University of California Press, 1975), p. 40. For other discussions of the masque as a courtly form, see Malcolm Smuts, *Court Culture And The Origins of A Royalist Tradition in Early Stuart England* (Philadelphia: University of Pennsylvania Press, 1987), chap. 9, and Kevin Sharpe, *Criticism And Compliment. The Politics of Literature in The England of Charles I* (Cambridge: Cambridge University Press, 1987), chap. 5. Beside bringing out the distinctive features of *Comus*, Brown also discusses the significance of some of the differences between the manuscript versions and the first printed edition of the poem in 1637 (which was published by Henry Lawes without the author's name), insofar as these may throw light on its intention. Maryann C. McGuire, *Milton's Puritan Masque* (Athens: University of Georgia Press, 1983), stresses the contrasts between *Comus* and other masques. Although conceivable, as she argues, that the work may have been related to the contemporary controversy over sabbath observance and Sunday sports which was provoked by Puritan opposition to James I's Declaration

Comus was composed as an entertainment in honor of John Egerton, earl of Bridgewater, Lord President of The Council in Wales, and was first performed at Ludlow Castle on 29 September 1634 in the presence of Bridgewater and his wife and guests as part of the festivities to celebrate his visit to his presidency, to which Charles I had appointed him three years before. The earl was the countess dowager of Derby's step-son and also her son-in-law by his marriage to one of her daughters. This family relationship explains Henry Lawes's association with the occasion, and it must have been because of him that Milton was asked to write the work. Beside acting the part of the Attendant Spirit, Lawes staged the masque and composed its music. Bridgewater's three youngest children also took part in the performance, the fifteen year old Lady Alice as the Lady, and her two brothers, Lord Brackley, age eleven, and Thomas Egerton, age nine, in the roles of the Elder and the Younger Brother.[42]

Rich in the mythological imagery of the pagan world and in exquisite echoes of Latin poetry, Shakespeare, and Spenser, *Comus* is a moral drama exhibiting the high level of character and conduct Milton demanded of noble rank. In sketching the scene at the play's beginning, the Attendant Spirit notes its occasion in a compliment to Bridgewater, entrusted by the king with the government of Wales and the border counties:

> And all this tract that fronts the falling sun
> A noble peer of mickle trust, and power
> Has in his charge, with tempered awe to guide
> An old, and haughty nation proud in arms:
> Where his fair offspring nursed in princely lore
> Are coming to attend their father's state,
> And new-entrusted sceptre.... (30–36)

---

of Sports in 1618 and its reissue in 1633 by Charles I, there are no specific references in the text to support this unlikely view.

[42] Brown, chaps. 1–2, gives the details concerning the genesis of *Comus* and its connection with the Bridgewater family. Barbara Breasted, "*Comus* And The Castlehaven Scandal," *Milton Studies*, vol. III (1971), and several other scholars have implausibly connected the theme of chastity in *Comus* with the trial and execution in 1631 of the earl of Castlehaven for rape, sodomy and other infamous offenses. Castlehaven was another of the countess dowager's sons-in-law and hence also related to the earl of Bridgewater's family. No evidence exists, however, to indicate that Milton, if he knew about the Castlehaven scandal, which was not unlikely, had it in mind in writing *Comus*, and it is inconceivable that he would have wished to remind his audience of it, however indirectly; see also Brown's comments, pp. 175–177.

The moral challenge in the poem takes the classic form of a quest or journey by the nobleman's children to find their parents, during which the Lady confronts and resists the temptations presented by Comus, child of Circe and incarnation of sensuality and disorder. Armed with chastity, she is invulnerable to his invitation to sexual enjoyment. At his offer of a cup to assuage her thirst, she refuses lest it contain a dangerous potion of "Liquorish baits":

> Were it a draught for Juno when she banquets,
> I would not taste thy treasonous offer; none
> But such as are good men can give good things,
> And that which is not good, is not delicious
> To a well-governed and wise appetite.   (700–705)

Nor is she deceived by Comus's libertine argument that Nature commands beauty to fulfill itself in feasting and sexual pleasure, and insists in her reply that self-discipline is Nature's rule:

> Imposter do not charge most innocent Nature,
> As if she would her children should be riotous
> With her abundance she good cateress
> Means her provision only to the good
> That live according to her sober laws,
> And holy dictate of spare temperance: (761–766)

The Elder Brother similarly eulogizes chastity and lauds the power of virtue, which

> may be assailed, but never hurt,
> Surprised by unjust force, but not enthralled,
> Yea even that which mischief meant most harm
> Shall in the happy trial prove most glory.   (588–591)

Consciousness of degree and aristocratic social responsibility pervades the poem. The Lady reveals the fastidiousness of her breeding at the outset when, lost in the wood, she seeks to avoid "the sound of riot, and ill-managed merriment" of "loose, unlettered hinds." (171–173). To the offer of help from Comus disguised as a shepherd, she replies with gracious condescension:

> Shepherd I take thy word,
> And trust they honest-offered courtesy,
> Which oft is sooner found in lowly sheds
> With smoky rafters, than in tap'stry halls
> And courts of princes, where it first was named,
> And yet is most pretended: (321–325).

27

These sentiments are devoid of radical import and belong to the expected rhetoric of pastoral reflecting the conventional notion of the virtues of simple country folk. Equally conventional is the Lady's subsequent condemnation of surfeit and her praise of temperance:

> If every just man that now pines with want
> Had but a moderate and beseeming share
> Of that which lewdly-pampered Luxury
> Now heaps upon some few with vast excess,
> Nature's full blessing would be well-disposed
> In unsuperfluous even proportion,.... (767–772)

The critical sting in this passage takes its force from the traditional ideal of aristocratic paternalism and its corollary, the reciprocal obligations of a moral community in which those of high station acknowledge responsibility for the welfare of its poorer and weaker members. Its import does not differ from Gloucester's injunction in *King Lear* that "distribution should undo excess, And each man have enough."[43]

The masque's conclusion highlights the motifs of nobility and virtue and their accord. After leading the three children to their parents at Ludlow Castle, the Attendant Spirit sings of their achievement:

> Noble Lord, and Lady Bright,
> I have brought ye new delight,
> Here behold so goodly grown
> Three fair branches of your own,
> Heaven hath timely tried their youth,
> Their faith, their patience, and their truth,
> And sent them here through hard assays
> With a crown of deathless praise,
> To triumph in victorious dance
> O'er sensual folly and intemperance. (965–974)

The Attendant Spirit's final verse sums up the moral:

> Mortals that would follow me
> Love virtue, she alone is free,
> She can teach ye how to climb
> Higher than the sphery chime;
> Or if virtue feeble were,
> Heaven itself would stoop to her. (1017–1022)

---

[43] *King Lear*, IV, 1, 70–71; see the editor's note to the passage in *Comus* cited above, CF, p. 215n.

Comus tells us a good deal about Milton's mind in the 1630s amid the seeming stability of England's polity which was shortly to give way to revolution. The poem conveys an ardent moral idealism that is nonetheless generally consistent with the decorum demanded by the particular occasion of tribute to a nobleman for which it was written. It does not imply in any way that the poet felt at odds with his society; but in keeping with his strongly felt sense of vocation, he uses it to teach a lesson. The markedly didactic note in *Comus* exemplifies the author's conception of the values requisite to a true and godly aristocracy such as he wished his own country's to be. These values – self-discipline, justice, social responsibility, avoidance of luxury and sexual irregularity – would not have have been unfamiliar to his audience; they were the same ones that many religious teachers and moralists sought to inculcate in the members of the English governing class. Milton, so intensely conscious of his own personal distinction, focuses on the qualities proper to an elite entrusted with the moral and political leadership of a nation.[44] This subject was always one of his foremost concerns, and it constitutes a consistent and continuing thread in his political thought throughout the many changes he was to experience in the years ahead.

[44] Donald M. Friedman, "*Comus* And The Truth of The Ear," in "*The Muses Common-Weale.*" *Poetry And Politics in The Seventeenth Century*, ed. Claude J. Summers and Ted-Larry Pebworth (Columbia: University of Missouri Press, 1988), discusses a number of recent interpretations of *Comus*, some of which try to extract from it an explicit religious and political criticism of the existing order. My own understanding of *Comus* accords broadly with Brown's interpretation, chaps. 1, 7, and passim, which is valuable for its insight and convincing historical placement of the work. I think, however, that he exaggerates considerably in describing *Comus* as insistently prescribing the reformation of England's leading class. I can find no evidence, moreover, for his view that haemony, the medicinal drug which enables the Attendant Spirit to see through Comus's enchantments and disguises, and which he promises to give to the Elder Brother (617–647), stands for the word of God.

29

Chapter 2

MILTON IN REVOLUTION:
EPISCOPACY, DIVORCE, UNLICENSED PRINTING

The assembling of the Long Parliament on 3 November 1640 opened an era of unprecedented experiment and revolutionary change in England's history. As the revolt against the Stuart monarchy grew, it brought on a civil war in 1642 that swept away ancient institutions and gave rise to radical new conceptions of political, religious, and social freedom. Traditional authority in church and state disintegrated, creating a vast ferment of thought and battle of ideas which brought many inherited beliefs and assumptions into question. From the outset of the conflict Milton took his stand with the popular and parliamentary forces aligned against the Stuart regime and ecclesiastical hierarchy. The middle period of his life coincided with the two decades of the revolution, to which he gave many of his best energies. He was an active partisan in some of its principal events and was intensely affected by its hopes, victories, and ultimate defeat.

The Long Parliament met with the determination to put an end to the absolutism of Charles I's government during the preceding years. Its first actions were to punish the ministers who had been the instruments of royal misrule and to pass measures imposing new limits on the powers of the crown in order to assure the future existence and authority of parliament and the supremacy of law. At the same time it was forced to include religious reform on its agenda owing to the bitter hostility engendered by the Arminian policies and harsh ecclesiastical administration of Archbishop Laud and his episcopal coadjutors. With the cessation of the government's ability to enforce censorship, an explosion of public discussion took place in press and pulpit. From all parts of the kingdom petitions poured into parliament calling for the redress of grievances in church and state. Separatist sects likewise came into being demanding toleration, claiming the right of unordained laymen and even of women to preach, and alarming the orthodox with their heretical opinions. While Puritan ministers inveighed against the misdeeds of the past and greeted the dawn of a new day of reformation, the press poured out an ever-increasing flood of publications concerned with current political and religious issues.

It was in this suddenly transformed political atmosphere, of which London was the focal point, that Milton made his debut as a pamphleteer. Between May 1641 and April 1642 he published five pamphlets, all but one anonymously, advocating the abolition of episcopacy. The issue of church government had come into the spotlight through a petition presented to the House of Commons in December 1640 in behalf of 15,000 Londoners. Blaming episcopacy as the cause of many evils, the signers called for its removal "with all its dependencies, roots and branches," and its replacement by church government "according to God's Word...." The Root and Branch Petition provoked a storm of controversy and a swarm of publications followed in the succeeding months defending and condemning episcopacy. Among them was an attack on bishops issued in March 1641 by five Puritan ministers who collectively signed themselves "Smectymnuus," a pseudonym composed of their initials. Its main author was Milton's former tutor, Thomas Young. In May Milton joined the battle on the same side with his first pamphlet, *Of Reformation Touching Church-Discipline in England*, and this and the four works that ensued form a sequence of exchanges with the adversaries of his position.[1]

Milton's anti-prelatical tracts are considerably more significant as a revelation of his state of mind in 1641–42 than as an expression of political thought. While exceptional in their rhetorical power, their political ideas were unremarkable, serving merely to reinforce his indictment of bishops. If there was anything novel in them, it was in their blazing hopes and expectations. Regarding the subject of episcopacy itself, he had nothing original or different to offer. What he had to say did not compare in practical knowledge or political acuteness with the writings of some of the other opponents of the

---

[1] The Root and Branch petition is printed in S. R. Gardiner, *Constitutional Documents of The Puritan Revolution 1625–1660*, 3rd rev. ed. (Oxford: Clarendon Press, 1936), pp. 137–144. The tract by Smectymnuus, *An Answer to A Book, Entituled, An Humble Remonstrance*, was a reply to a defense of episcopacy by Joseph Hall bishop of Norwich. Don M. Wolfe's introduction to CPW, vol. I, surveys the context of controversy to which Milton's anti-episcopal pamphlets belonged. See also the discussion of their character in J. W. Allen, *English Political Thought 1603–1660* (London: Methuen, 1938), pt. V, chap. IV, and William Haller, *The Rise of Puritanism* (New York: Columbia University Press, 1938), pp. 344–363.

bishops, such as Lord Brooke's *A Discourse Opening The Nature of That Episcopacy Which Is Exercized in England*, published in November 1641 at the height of the controversy. There is no sign that his pamphlets attracted much attention or affected the nature of the debate. So great was his dislike of episcopacy that he was incapable of judging it fairly while exposing its faults. He treated the subject with the utmost prejudice, leveling unfounded accusations, caricaturing history and indulging in wild exaggerations, and insulting his opponents by rude personal attacks.

All of the anti-prelatical tracts were an impassioned plea for a great national reformation of religion. Their main theme was that episcopacy survived as a corrupt encumbrance from the past which must be discarded in order to complete the long deferred and scarcely begun reformation that had come to a halt in Queen Elizabeth's reign. Milton now perceived the imminence of this reformation, with which, as his autobiographical statements show, he also identified the fulfillment of his own promise to write a great epic poem. Although recognizing some of the obstacles in the way, he was convinced that God had singled out England above all other nations to become a holy community and example of Christian renewal. It is evident that recent events had moved him profoundly and caused him to entertain the highest hopes. He felt himself to be living in "an age of ages wherein God is manifestly come downe among us, to doe some remarkable good to our Church or state."[2] He was far from alone in this mood of apocalyptic fervor. Many Puritans felt it and it also found vehement expression in the sermons well known Puritan preachers like Stephen Marshall and Cornelius Burges delivered before the House of Commons.[3] In Milton, however, this state of mind attained a unique intensity through the power of his imagination and his passionate idealism.

At this juncture he resembled other Puritan authors like Smectymnuus in giving his allegiance to a presbyterian type of church polity which had its origins in Calvin's Geneva and was already established in revolutionary Scotland. Instead of the Anglican hierarchy ruled by bishops, he urged church government by ministers or presbyters and elders in parish consistories and

[2] *Animadversions upon The Remonstrants Defence against Smectymnuus*, 1641, CPW, vol. I, p. 705. David Loewenstein, *Milton And The Drama of History* (Cambridge: Cambridge University Press, 1990), chap. 1, contains an interesting discussion of Milton's anti-prelatical tracts which relates them to his dramatic and apocalyptic vision of history as turbulent and violent, a theme he follows through a number of the poet's subsequent works during and after the revolution.

[3] See John F. Wilson, *Pulpit in Parliament* (Princeton: Princeton University Press, 1969).

provincial and national assemblies. Although vague about the details of this structure, which he outlined somewhat more fully in *The Reason of Church-Government* than in his other tracts, he held that it was the only one prescribed in Scripture and that its establishment was essential to reformation. He spoke of it as discipline, the same term Calvin and the English Puritans used to designate one of the prerequisites of a true visible church.[4] For him the concept of discipline possessed an exceptionally ample meaning. It represented the principle of order both within and without. On the one hand, it denoted the external order of the church framed according to Scripture, which teaches saving doctrine, keeps people from sin, and admonishes, reclaims and punishes offenders against moral and divine law. On the other hand, it signified the internal order of virtue based on personal self-command. The two were interconnected and mutually reinforcing. Although Milton was to reject Presbyterianism before long and eventually ceased to believe in any visible church, the necessity of discipline in the individual and society remained one of his cardinal moral and political tenets. In *The Reason of Church-Government*, he pronounced a great encomium on discipline which indicates the large place it occupied in his mind. He praised it as vital to the entire life of man. It was "not only the removall of disorder," but the "very visible shape and image" of "divine things" and of "virtue." Every "sociable perfection...civill or sacred," he held, the flourishing and decay of nations and commonwealths, and all human affairs depend on discipline, for it is "she...that with...her musicall cords preserves and holds all parts...together." Even the angels, "distinguisht and quaterniond into their celestiall Princedomes and Satrapies," and the state of the blessed in paradise, are subject to discipline. He could not conceive, he concluded, that God would have left his beloved church on earth "to the perpetual stumble of conjecture and disturbance without the card and Compasse of Discipline."[5]

Beside the importance he assigned to discipline, another prominent note in the anti-prelatical tracts was his contemptuous attitude toward the past. In claiming that the New Testament prescribed the sole model of a church, he spurned the authority of antiquity, custom, and precedent in favor of reliance exclusively on Scripture.

---

[4] John Calvin, *Institutes of The Christian Religion*, 2 vols., ed. J. T. McNeill (Philadelphia: Westminster Press, 1960), vol. II, bk. IV, chap. 12, and the editor's introduction, vol. I, pp. lxi–lxiii; *An Admonition to Parliament*, 1572, in *Puritan Manifestoes*, ed. W. H. Frere and C. E. Douglas (London: S. P. C. K., 1954), p. 9.

[5] *The Reason of Church-Government Urg'd against Prelaty*, 1642, CPW, vol. I, pp. 751–753.

To him the votaries of antiquity were "hinderers of Reformation," and though forced to use historical arguments in disputing with episcopacy's defenders about its role in the early church and the opinions of the church fathers, he maintained that even the latters' times were "fouly tainted." As he conceived it, Christianity after the period of Christ and the apostles had declined into a long night of corruption and error not lifted until, with the advent of Wyclif and the Protestant reformers, "the bright and Blissful Reformation" broke through the darkness of "Ignorance and Antichristian tyranny...."[6] Terming custom a "tyrant," he denied that old ways need be good ways or that "either God or nature...divine or Humane wisdom" ever intended men to make antiquity their rule in deciding any weighty doctrine. Why, then, he inquired, should they stand "worshipping and admiring this...livelesse Colossus," when God had given them Scripture as a just and adequate measure of truth?[7] While Milton's reasoning in this context related only to the nature of the church, he couched his dismissal of the authority of antiquity in such broad terms that it could easily come to serve as a critical principle in the political realm as well.

In the more explicit political observations in the anti-prelatical tracts, the moral standpoint predominated. The "art of policie," Milton contended, should aim "to train up a Nation in true wisdom...vertue and...godlines" which make up "the true florishing of a Land." Modern politicians, on the contrary, had sought instead to subject the people to oppression and rapine and to corrupt their national spirit through luxury and ignorance.[8] He denounced the bishops as instruments of tyranny pernicious to both king and people. They were usurpers of royal power as well as enemies of the liberty of the subject guilty of trampling laws and statutes under foot, grasping after wealth and worldly employments, and slighting the "indiminishable Majestie of our highest Court the Law-Giving and Sacred Parliament."[9] He made a strenuous effort to counter the common opinion of episcopacy's proponents that only the institution of bishops was compatible with monarchy. In reply he maintained that church government need not conform to civil polity and that bishops tended to the destruction of monarchy, while presbyterian discipline by its moral supervision and avoidance of meddling in

[6] *Of Reformation Touching Church-Discipline in England*, 1641, CPW, vol. I, pp. 524, 541, 549.

[7] *The Reason of Church-Government*, p. 853; *Animadversions upon The Remonstrants Defence against Smectymnuus*, 1641, CPW, vol. I, pp. 698, 699.

[8] *Of Reformation*, pp. 571–572.

[9] Ibid., pp. 592–593.

temporal affairs would lend support to magistracy and render the people more quiet and easily governable.[10]

As yet Milton evinced no trace of hostility to monarchy as such. After observing, in accord with a familiar classical doctrine, that the best-founded commonwealths have aimed at "a certaine mixture or temperament" partaking of the virtues of several forms of states, he commended the excellency of England's government above all others because it is "equally balanc'd...by the hand and scale of Justice...." In it, he said,

> under a free, and untutor'd Monarch, the noblest, worthiest, and most prudent men, with full approbation, and suffrage of the People, have in their power the supreame, and finall determination of highest Affairs.[11]

He thus took the view that England's was a mixed government composed of the three ingredients of kingship, aristocracy, and people. It is not clear where he derived this conception, but he could have easily picked up its elements from several sixteenth-century authors, most probably from Sir Thomas Smith's *De Republica Anglorum*.[12]

He also bestowed a fulsome panegyric on the parliament, which he quite unrealistically glorified. It was impossible, he thought, to praise its members too highly for their noble deeds. They were both reformers of the church and restorers of the commonwealth who had won back the nation's "lost liberties and charters, which our forefathers after so many battels could scarce maintaine," and had also slain the second life of tyranny in the form of prelacy. Saluting them as "Fathers of their Countrey," he described how they "sit as gods among daily Petitions and publick thanks flowing in upon them," and the courtesy with which they received the complaints of "the meanest artizans and labourers, at other times also women, and often the younger sort of servants...." The idealistic exaggeration of these comments pervaded by reminiscences of classical and Roman history is noteworthy. He was equally at pains to emphasize parliament's aristocratic character, and pointed out that most of its members were "either of ancient and high Nobility, or at least of

---

[10] Ibid., pp. 573–577.

[11] Ibid., p. 599.

[12] See Michael Mendle, *Dangerous Positions* (n. p.: University of Alabama Press, 1985), chap. 3, which discusses sixteenth-century English concepts of mixed government. Milton was familiar with the idea from classical sources such as Polybius, whom he cites in *Of Reformation*, p. 599. He cites Sir Thomas Smith in his *Commonplace Book*. On this subject see also Zera S. Fink, *The Classical Republicans* (Evanston: Northwestern University Press, 1945), pp. 95–96.

knowne and well reputed ancestry, which is a great advantage towards virtue," although also presenting temptations to wealth, ease, and flattery which they had overcome.[13]

In this exhilarating atmosphere, the immense hopefulness with which he embraced parliament also extended to the people. Like revolutionary artists and intellectuals in France after 1789, Soviet Russia after 1917, and Red China after 1949, he strongly idealized the people, professing the fullest confidence in its wisdom. Enthusiastically in favor of the popular election of ministers, he was sure that "the meanest Christians" reared on the scriptures were as capable as any bishop of judging Christ's doctrine and discerning a good from a bad minister. He could see no reason why "a plaine artizan" should be denied a voice in choosing his minister as if incompetent to decide.[14] He took a charitable view of newly born religious groups, brushing aside the fear of sects and schisms as a specter raised by the defenders of episcopacy to defame reformation. Just as Lollards and Hussites were once terms of abuse, so now, he cautioned, were the names Puritan and Brownist. Sects and divisions, however, were inevitable in the reforming of the church, "which is never brought to effect without the fierce encounter of truth and falshood together...." He was confident that "when truth has the upper hand and the reformation shall be perfected," then "many fond errors and fanatick opinions will easily be rid out of the way...."[15]

All of these beliefs coalesced in a recurrent theme of the antiprelatical tracts, the overwhelming conviction that God had appointed England to be his protagonist in a cosmic struggle for reformation. Milton perceived the English as an elect nation bound to God by covenant like Israel of old.[16] In a vehement outpouring of prayer recalling how God had preserved his country from the peril of the Spanish Armada, he uttered profound thanks for past deliverances from anti-Christian thralldom and greater happiness still to come.[17] He knew that God, though equally near the whole creation,

---

[13] *An Apology against A Pamphlet Call'd A Modest Confutation*, 1642, CPW, vol. I, pp. 922–926.

[14] Ibid., p. 933.

[15] *The Reason of Church-Government*, pp. 783–785, 788, 795–796.

[16] This patriotic Protestant theme had been given a historical grounding and become widely popular through the famous work of the Elizabethan church historian, John Foxe's *Acts and Monuments* (The Book of Martyrs), first published in 1563 and then in many later editions, which may have influenced Milton; see William Haller, *Foxe's Book of Martyrs and the Elect Nation* (London: Jonathan Cape, 1963), pp. 238–242.

[17] *Of Reformation*, pp. 614–615.

"hath yet ever had this Land under the speciall indulgent eye of his providence; and pittying us the first of all other Nations," had there begun the purification of his church. He implored divine assistance in leading his countrymen to complete the blessed work of reformation; though God had previously visited England, "the power of thy grace is not past away with the primitive times, as fond and faithless men imagine, but thy Kingdom is now at hand, and thou standing at the dore."[18]

It was with this vast expectation of a glorious future that Milton greeted the first years of the English revolution. Through some of the autobiographical passages in the anti-prelatical tracts, he made himself part of this future as the elect poet who promised to sing the greatness of his nation and the beneficence of God. Despite having to contend against the obduracy of the defenders of episcopacy, he had experienced nothing yet to undermine his faith. He showed little interest thus far in the question of liberty, which he conceived primarily as a moral quality. "Well knowes every wise Nation," he commented in *Of Reformation*,

> that their Liberty consists in manly and honest labours, in sobriety and rigorous honor to the marriage bed....and when the people slacken, and fall to looseness, and riot, then doe they as much as if they laid down their necks for some wily Tyrant to get up and ride.[19]

A strong strain of anti-clericalism entered into his dislike of bishops. His pride and the reverence he felt for himself as "a fit person to do the noblest and godliest deeds," made him bitterly resent the episcopal order's claim to superiority, and he assailed the presumption of a usurping clergy who make the term "Laick" a thing of scorn.[20] Lacking any familiarity with the working of the presbyterian polity, his conception of it was highly unrealistic. He insisted that the church must possess "no jurisdictive power," thereby leaving unexplained how it was to enforce its spiritual censures.[21] Convinced that it would abstain from involvement in temporal matters, he took no account, in spite of many recent historical examples in Protestant Europe, of the conflicts that could arise between it and the secular authority. He idealized its discipline, censures, and excommunication as paternal, mild, and tender, intolerable only to libertines, never considering that its pressures for conformity could have a stifling

---

18 *Animadversions*, pp. 704, 706, 707.
19 *Of Reformation*, p. 588.
20 *The Reason of Church-Government*, pp. 842, 843.
21 Ibid., pp. 832, 834.

effect on freedom of conscience.[22] As yet he was naively ignorant that the Presbyterian church government he recommended so warmly might be as theocratic and susceptible to clericalism as was the episcopal church he detested, and that "a pope in every parish," a concern he blithely dismissed, could be as repressive as a bishop in a diocese.[23]

Milton published his final pamphlet against episcopacy in April 1642. Two months later he became a married man. His wife, Mary Powell, was the oldest daughter of Richard Powell, a gentleman residing at Forest Hill in Oxfordshire, who in 1627 had borrowed three hundred pounds from the elder Milton, a debt which the latter afterward transferred to his son as an investment. Milton met Mary Powell in June, when he journeyed to Oxfordshire to see about the interest on the loan, which was in danger of arrears because of her father's financial troubles. It is obvious that he was immediately smitten by the seventeen-year old girl and impetuously married her. The newly-wed couple then came back with a number of her relatives to his London house for some further days of celebration of their nuptials. When these ended and her relations departed, Mary, who had grown up in a large, lively household, was left solitary and ill-at-ease with a much older husband of strict, studious habits. Milton had not only his studies to occupy him, but also his work as tutor of his two young nephews, Edward and John Phillips, whom he was educating. After a few weeks he acceded to her request to be allowed to make a short visit to her home. When the end of September passed without her return as promised, he sent for her by letter and messenger, all to no avail. Milton found himself to be a deserted husband, and his resentment was aggravated by the fact that the Powells were Royalists. Throughout the spring and summer of 1642 the prospect of civil war between the king and parliament came steadily nearer, as all attempts to achieve a political compromise failed. By the end of August, the two parties were engaged in raising armies, and the king had proclaimed his opponents as traitors and rebels against his lawful power. Edgehill, the first battle of the civil war, took place on 23 October, and a few days later Charles I occupied Oxford, which remained his headquarters for the duration of the conflict. With the outbreak of hostilities, communications between London and Oxfordshire, a Royalist area, became very difficult. On their side, moreover, the Powells, who were ardent

[22] *Of Reformation*, pp. 570, 591.
[23] Ibid., p. 570.

Royalists, regretted their daughter's marriage to a supporter of parliament, and their political antipathy helped perpetuate the separation.[24]

It is impossible to overestimate the effect on Milton of his wife's desertion. As one of his early biographers, perhaps his nephew, John Phillips, described it, he "was then in the full Vigor of his Manhood" and "could ill bear the disappointment he met with by her obstinate absenting...."[25] Although he avoided the slightest direct reference to the failure of his marriage in any of his writings, his anger and humiliation are apparent from numerous unmistakable allusions in his divorce tracts. Not only did his wife's rejection wound and incense him, but he knew he had made a disastrous blunder that he could not rectify, since English law prohibited divorce for any reason except adultery. This meant that he could neither cast off his disloyal spouse nor remarry.

The divorce tracts were his personal response to this acutely painful situation. Between August 1643 and March 1645 he published four pamphlets in favor of divorce on the ground of incompatibility of mind and temper. The first, *The Doctrine And Discipline of Divorce*, appeared again a few months later in an enlarged edition. It was followed by *The Judgement of Martin Bucer Concerning Divorce, Tetrachordon*, and the last, *Colasterion*, a reply to a pamphlet opposing his views. Looking back on them a decade later, he chose to represent them as a plea for domestic liberty which he had deliberately undertaken as part of a systematic design following his defense of ecclesiastical liberty in his anti-prelatical tracts.[26] At the time, though, they were surely not the result of any plan, but the product of an urgent psychological and moral need. He felt bound to overcome the defeat of his desertion. The necessity to justify himself and to erase his failure by rationalizing and objectifying his personal plight, compelled him to examine the nature of marriage in order to define the true conditions which should morally and legally permit its dissolution.

The divorce tracts marked a decisive breakthrough in Milton's

[24] Parker, vol. I, pp. 229–232, recounts the story of Milton's marriage, and some vivid details which are probably authentic are included in the biography of Milton by his nephew, Edward Phillips, *The Life of Mr. John Milton*, in *The Early Lives of John Milton*, ed. Helen Darbishire (London: Constable, 1932), pp. 63–65.

[25] John Phillips, *The Life of Mr. John Milton*, in *The Early Lives of Milton*, p. 23. The editor, Helen Darbishire, has attributed this anonymous biography to John Phillips, pp. xvi–xix; Parker, vol. I, pp. xiii–xv, discusses other attributions and argues that its author was Cyriack Skinner, one of Milton's pupils.

[26] *A Second Defence of The English People*, CPW, vol. IV, pt. 1, p. 624.

development as a radical and rebel. In his tracts against episcopacy he had written as part of the Puritan mainstream and had actually endorsed, for his own naive reasons, what he soon came to realize was a repressive ecclesiastical system. In his attitude to divorce he stood virtually alone as the advocate of a broad liberty of ending marriage, a position requiring exceptional intellectual courage to maintain. Although his discussion of divorce was not directly related to politics, some of the concepts he employed stemmed from political sources and were rich in political implication. For the first time a new set of ideas such as contract, equity, the law of nature, and liberty, which were to occupy a central position in his political thought, made its appearance in his work.

The divorce tracts exerted little influence. The notice they attracted was due almost wholly to the scandal their unconventional opinions aroused. It was this reaction that led Milton to bid farewell to Presbyterianism. On this subject also he never said a word to admit that he had changed his opinion or been mistaken in his former support of Presbyterian church government. The Presbyterian clergy's condemnation of his views, however, was among the causes that made the break inevitable. Preachers before parliament called for the suppression of his work as wicked and immoral. He was described as an impudent, licentious author and proponent of sexual promiscuity. Even his old tutor, Thomas Young, joined the chorus, warning in a sermon to the House of Commons against legalizing "digamy."[27] Milton was surprised and indignant at these misrepresentations. From this and other evidence his eyes were opened to the Presbyterians' intolerance, and his estrangement followed. By 1644, if not sooner, he had become their adversary, seeing them as the embodiment of a new ecclesiastical tyranny and joining the opposition to their attempt to persuade parliament to impose a compulsory presbyterian system of church government on the nation which would deny freedom of conscience to dissenters from its rule. Beside his subsequent prose writings, two poems of 1646 gave trenchant expression to his rejection of the Presbyterians and their church polity. In the first, aimed against the detractors of his divorce tracts, he pictured himself as an exponent of truth who

> ...did but prompt the age to quit their clogs
> By the known rules of ancient liberty,

---

[27] Milton's divorce tracts are printed in CPW, vol. II. Ernest Sirluck, the volume's editor, describes their occasion and the reaction to them, pp. 137–145; see also Parker, vol. I, pp. 263–264, for details of the reaction.

and was promptly environed by "a barbarous noise...Of owls and cuckoos, asses, apes, and dogs."[28] The second, "On The New Forcers of Conscience under The Long Parliament," condemned the Presbyterians for urging the use of the civil sword "to force our consciences that Christ set free," and bitingly concluded that "New Presbyter is but Old Priest writ large."

The degree to which Milton's motives in writing his divorce tracts mirrored his own domestic misfortune is evident from many passages in them. His purpose was to free spouses, and the husband in particular, from the intolerable fetter of a failed, unhappy marriage. He clearly had himself in mind in *The Doctrine And Discipline of Divorce* when he demanded "some conscionable and tender pitty" for "those who have unwarily in a thing they never practiz'd before, made themselves the bondmen of a luckles and helpless matrimony." "...it may yet befall a discreet man," he likewise observed, "to be mistaken in his choice: and we have plenty of examples," for "the soberest and best govern'd men are lest practiz'd" in the affair of marriage. Nor is it especially strange, he added, that "many who have spent their youth chastly, are in some things not so quick-sighted, while they hast too eagerly to light the nuptial torch...."[29] Elsewhere he pointed out that "the best and wisest men amidst the sincere and most cordiall designes of their heart doe dayly erre in choosing" their wives.[30] "To men of quality," he stated in the last of the divorce tracts, "I have said anough, and experience confirms by daily example, that wisest, sobrest, justest men are somtimes miserably mistak'n in their chois. Whom to leave thus without remedy, tost and tempested in a most unquiet sea of afflictions and temptations...is most unchristianly."[31]

As was his wont, however, he gave to these personal considerations a universal significance by absorbing them into his consciousness of vocation as one divinely inspired to champion freedom of divorce as a mission of liberation. He felt himself to be "the sole advocate of a discount'nanc't truth," a man engaged in "a high enterprise and a hard, and such as every seventh Son of a seventh Son does not venture on." Yet if one "be gifted with abilities of mind," he said of himself, "that may raise him to so high an undertaking,"

[28] *Sonnet XII*, "On The Detraction Which Followed Upon My Writing Certain Treatises," CF, p. 295.

[29] *The Doctrine And Discipline of Divorce*, pp. 240, 249. The text in CPW conflates both the 1643 and 1644 editions of this work.

[30] *Tetrachordon*, p. 598.

[31] *Colasterion*, p. 742.

then there was nothing to repent. He trusted that "through the help of that illuminating Spirit which hath favor'd me," he had established the true doctrine of divorce and thus removed great difficulties "which have hitherto molested the Church of God...to the unspeakable good of Christendom."[32] That he had found out this truth alone, with only infallible Scripture as his guide, he did not doubt. He was "no other then a passive instrument under some power and counsel higher and better than can be human," receiving "no light, or leading...from any man." God, it seemed, "intended to prove me whether I durst alone take up a rightful cause against a world of disesteem, & found I durst."[33] To parliament, moreover, to which he dedicated the first three of the four divorce tracts, he renewed his promise of an immortal future work. "I have yet a store of gratitude laid up," he avowed, "which cannot be exhausted; and such thanks perhaps they may live to be, as shall more than whisper to the next ages."[34]

The heart of Milton's case in the divorce tracts was that God did not institute matrimony primarily to legitimate sexual intercourse as a remedy against sin, nor even chiefly for the purpose of procreation, but for the sake of mutual companionship and the relief of loneliness as its supreme end.[35] His ideal of marriage subordinated its sexual side, which he characterized in such contemptuous phrases as "the prescrib'd satisfaction of an irrationall heat," "a bestiall necessity" and "sublunary and bestial burning," and "the promiscuous draining of a carnall rage." Marital sex without love and peace meant nothing more than "to grind in the mill of an undelighted and servil copulation...."[36] Above the physical relationship in marriage he placed "the apt and cheerful conversation of man with woman to comfort and refresh him against the evill of a solitary life," and "the amiable and attractive society of conjugall love, beside the deed of procreation, which of it self soon cloies...unless it bee cherisht and re-incited with a pleasing conversation."[37] By conversation he did not mean only the friendly exchange of talk, but the agreement of mind and feeling essential to marital union. Without "the sweet and mild familiarity of love and solace and mutual fitness...and meet help," matrimony was like a body without a soul.[38] This was the basis for

---

[32] *The Doctrine And Discipline of Divorce*, pp. 224, 340.
[33] *The Judgement of Martin Bucer*, pp. 433, 434.
[34] *Tetrachordon*, p. 579.
[35] *The Doctrine And Discipline of Divorce*, pp. 235, 246.
[36] Ibid., pp. 249, 258, 259–260, 269, 355.
[37] Ibid., p. 235; *Colasterion*, p. 740.
[38] *Tetrachordon*, p. 603.

his conviction that, far more than adultery, the strongest reason for divorce lay in "indisposition, unfitness, or contrariety of mind...hindring and ever likely to hinder the main benefits of conjugall society, which are solace and peace...." When spouses were in this condition, they should have the right to divorce and remarry if they please. He believed, moreover, that no civil or earthly power could have jurisdiction over this decision, which must depend entirely on the will and consent of both parties or of the husband alone.[39]

In urging this conclusion, Milton was obliged to undertake an exposition of various scriptural statements relating to marriage and divorce. Two texts in particular set the framework for his discussion. The first was the Mosaic law permitting a man to divorce his wife when he found some uncleanness in her (Deuteronomy 24:1). The second was Christ's reply to the Pharisees that Moses had granted divorce to the Jews solely because of their hardness of heart, but that it was allowable only for fornication, so that a man who put away his wife for any other cause and married another would be guilty of adultery (Matthew 19:3–9). Since in the Christian view the New Testament superseded and perfected the Old and the new law of the gospel took precedence over the old law in the Mosaic code, Milton had to show that Moses' permission of divorce still retained its validity and that there was no contradiction between it and Christ's injunction.[40] Against those who invoked Christ's words to prohibit divorce except for adultery he argued that Christ had never abrogated the Jewish moral law, as was evident from his pronouncement that not one jot or tittle of the law shall pass away while the world endures (Matthew 5:18); and further, that it was a rash and absurd imputation to suppose that Christ would have accused God's eternal law of countenancing the sin of adultery among the chosen people.[41] He praised the Mosaic law of divorce as prudent and full of equity, explaining that the hardness of heart it tolerated was its abuse by hypocrites, not its use by good men.[42] In expounding the nature of marriage, he also laid heavy stress on God's words of institution, "it is not good that man should be alone; I will make him a help meet for him" (Genesis 2:18), a decree signifying the priority of mutuality

[39] *The Doctrine And Discipline of Divorce*, pp. 242, 343–344; see also the discussion of Milton's conception of marriage and divorce in Edward Le Comte, *Milton And Sex* (London: Macmillan, 1978), chap. 2.

[40] These two texts figure considerably in *The Doctrine And Discipline of Divorce*, while *Tetrachordon* is almost entirely a work of scriptural exegesis expounding both these and a number of other passages bearing on marriage and divorce.

[41] *The Doctrine And Discipline of Divorce*, pp. 242–243, 250, 281–284.

[42] Ibid., pp. 306, 308.

43

help, and friendship in the marital relationship.[43] Correspondingly, he construed "uncleanness" in the passage in Deuteronomy to include various kinds of incompatibility as grounds for the dissolution of a marriage.[44] To Christ's statement to the Pharisees he attributed a restrictive meaning: it was intended specifically for them to bridle their licentiousness, not as a general denial of the remedy of divorce to good and blameless men.[45]

Within these interpretive strategies for dealing with the scriptural treatment of divorce Milton also introduced several normative considerations of far-reaching political import. He appealed to charity and equity as the underlying basis of all law, which therefore looks to the good of man as its sole end. Because laws needed to be understood in light of this end rather than with a strict literalism, it followed that Christ could not have ordained a law of divorce contrary to human good. "...who so preferrs either Matrimony," he said, "or other Ordinance before the good of man and the plain exigence of Charity, let him professe Papist, or Protestant, or what he will, he is no better then a Pharise, and understands not the Gospel...."[46] He applied the same reasoning to covenants. Like any ordinance, a covenant of marriage could have no force if, contrary to its end, it brought harm and misery to both parties.[47] Obviously, this principle might serve not only to liberalize the law of divorce, but to undermine any positive law or command and the arrangements it sanctioned. Milton gave it, moreover, virtually unlimited scope. "...no ordinance human or from heaven," he declared, "can binde against the good of man; so that to keep them strictly against that end, is all one with to breake them." Even more strikingly, he affirmed that "the great and almost only commandment of the Gospel, is to command nothing against the good of man, and much more no civil command, against his civil good."[48]

These ideas, springing from an extreme latitude of scriptural interpretation, represented a marked departure from the anti-episcopal tracts, in which Milton insisted on the literal prescriptive force of the New Testament model of the church. There can be little doubt that he owed them mainly to the publicists who defended parliament's political claims and its right of armed resistance against the king. With the approach and onset of the civil war, a fierce

[43] Ibid., pp. 308–309.
[44] Ibid., pp. 306–307.
[45] Ibid., pp. 282–283, 308–312.
[46] Ibid., p. 233.
[47] Ibid., p. 245; *Tetrachordon*, pp. 623–624.
[48] *Tetrachordon*, pp. 588, 638–639.

pamphlet combat broke out between parliament's apologists and Royalist propagandists who denounced parliament's program to control the king and its authorization of resistance as illegal and sinful. On the Parliamentarian side one of the leading authors was Henry Parker, whose *Observations upon Some of His Majesties Late Answers And Expresses* and other tracts made a powerful impression as the most persuasive statement in behalf of parliament and its supremacy over the king. Beside claiming that parliament as the representative body was identical with the people, Parker argued that political power and the authority of rulers derived from contract and the consent of the people, which are necessarily conditional. Rulers, therefore, whose power comes from the people, are obliged to use it for their welfare. "The Charter of Nature," Parker asserted, entitles all subjects to safety by its supreme law, and "there bee...tacite trusts and reservations in all publike commands, though of the most absolute nature that can be supposed." He likewise maintained that parliament alone was not only the proper interpreter of law in the case of disagreement with the king, but that the law need not be adhered to when it was inadequate to the preservation of the people.[49] Several Parliamentarian writers compared the covenants of marriage and of government in order to demonstrate that subjects might provide for their defense and safety in the same way that a husband or wife might separate from one another if wronged by adultery or violence.[50]

The close resemblance between these and Milton's reasonings is unmistakable. He made their political meaning explicit in a passage in the first of his divorce tracts which advanced an extreme version of the analogy between the contracts of marriage and subjection and the justification of their dissolution. Addressing parliament as "the supreme Senat," he asked how it could justify "the untainted honour" of its own actions if it excluded charity as the ground of law. "He who marries," he continued,

---

[49] Henry Parker, *Observations upon Some of His Majesties Late Answers And Expresses*, 1642, pp. 1, 4, 16; *The Contra-Replicant*, 1642, pp. 5–7, 19, cited in Margaret Judson, *The Crisis of The Constitution* (New Brunswick, N. J.: Rutgers University Press, 1949), p. 410.

[50] Several Parliamentarian pamphlets that advanced this analogy are discussed by Arthur E. Barker, *Milton And The Puritan Dilemma* (Toronto: The University of Toronto Press, 1942), pp. 108–110, and in Sirluck's introduction to CPW, vol. II, pp. 152–153. In *Tetrachordon*, p. 582, Milton mentioned his use of the principles put forward in one of these pamphlets, *Scripture And Reason Pleaded for Defensive Armes*, a justification by several ministers of parliament's right of resistance, which was published in April 1643.

intends as little to conspire his own ruine, as he that swears Allegiance: and as a whole people is in proportion to an ill Government, so is one man to an ill mariage. If they against any authority, Covnant, or Statute, may by the soveraign edict of charity, save not only their lives, but honest liberties from unworthy bondage, as well may he against any private Covnant, which hee never enter'd to his mischief, redeem himself from unsupportable disturbances to honest peace, and just contentment.[51]

That the political analogy of the marriage contract could also lend itself to the opposite conclusion, however, was made clear by a prominent Royalist who possibly had Milton's argument in mind. As in the case of marriage, he pointed out,

> so in Monarchy, there are two parties in the Contract; though without a mutuall agreement there could be no Covenant, yet after it is once made the dissent of the inferiour party, let it be not upon fancyed, but reall discontents, cannot dissolve the compact. Consent therefore joynd Man and Wife, King and People, but divine Ordinance continues this Union; Marriages and Governments both are ratified in heaven....whom God hath joynd, let not man put asunder; They must take their King for better for worse.'[52]

Beside subordinating divine and human law and contracts to the overriding equitable end of human good, Milton invoked the law of nature as another justifying principle. Thus he held that the prohibition of divorce to partners miserably yoked together would be contrary to the law of nature imprinted in human beings, which was of "more antiquity and deeper ground then marriage it selfe...." This law compelled individuals to shun harm and forbade laws to command against "the unreducible antipathies of nature...." Hence a law restraining divorce must violate the law of nature and nations.[53] Here the primordial law of nature dictating self-preservation and avoidance of injury became for Milton a norm standing over other enactments as their standard. To this law, moreover, the last of his divorce tracts added yet another, which he called "the secondary law of nature and nations," a concept he attributed to the Roman law. This secondary law regulated humanity after its fall from innocence

[51] *The Doctrine And Discipline of Divorce*, p. 229.

[52] Dudley Digges, *The Unlawfulnesse of Subjects Taking Up Armes against Their Soveraigne*, (London, 1st pub. 1644, 1647 ed.) p. 113.

[53] *The Doctrine And Discipline of Divorce*, pp. 237, 297, 342, 350; *Tetrachordon*, pp. 621–622. For this final conclusion Milton cites John Selden's recently published treatise on natural law, *De Jure Naturali et Gentium*, 1640; *The Doctrine And Discipline of Divorce*, p. 350.

into sin, and therefore tolerated such infirmities as hardness of heart and the inequalities of rich and poor. It also provided for divorce as well as marriage, "our imperfet and degenerat condition of necessity requiring this law among the rest, as a remedy against intolerable wrong and servitude above the patience of man to beare."[54]

It is useless to look for any coherence in Milton's discussion of these two laws of nature. He did not attempt to explain their coexistence or show how both could be equally binding; he simply brought them in as aids to support his general argument. Liberty was another principle on which he based his case for divorce. He wondered "why in this age many are so opposite both to human and to Christian liberty...contenting ...themselves in a specious humility and strictnesse bred out of low ignorance that never yet conceiv'd the freedom of the Gospel...."[55] First and foremost he had in mind Christian liberty, the gospel's gift to believers, which emancipated them from the burdensome observances and literalism of the law and made charity their rule. Christ did not introduce a new morality, but set men over the law and under the guidance of his living spirit. There was accordingly no reason why the gospel should deal so harshly with Christians as to deny them the privilege of divorce that the law granted to the Jews.[56] By analogy, the liberty of believers regenerated through Christ could also apply to human beings as rational creatures. This meant that "the reasonable Soul of man" could lay claim to a "just and honest liberty."[57] He even went so far as to offer the psychological suggestion that the aberrant behavior of the sectarian followers of anabaptism, antinomianism, and "other fanatick dreams," who were reputed to seek "satisfaction of the flesh," might be due to their being denied some lawful liberty which men ought to have.[58] Yet even with regard to this human liberty which he defended, Milton never shook off his predominant conviction that it rightly pertained only to those morally qualified. For this reason he also stressed that "just and naturall privileges man neither can rightly seek, nor dare fully claime, unless they be ally'd to inward goodnesse and stedfast knowledge," and that the liberty of divorce "was intended for good men principally, to bad only by accident."[59] Along with his growing concern for liberty both

54 *Tetrachordon*, pp. 661–662.
55 Ibid., p. 587.
56 *The Doctrine And Discipline of Divorce*, p. 304; *Tetrachordon*, pp. 587–588.
57 *The Doctrine And Discipline of Divorce*, p. 227.
58 Ibid., p. 278.
59 *Tetrachordon*, pp. 587, 621.

Christian and secular or human, Milton retained as strongly as ever his ethical bias and preoccupation with inward discipline and self-mastery in the service of virtue.[60]

Throughout his treatment of divorce, Milton, like all his contemporaries, assumed the natural superiority of the male, and therefore consistently accorded priority to the interests of the husband. Nevertheless, he did not wholly overlook the wife's concern in her freedom. *The Doctrine And Discipline of Divorce* bore the subtitle, "Restor'd to The Good of Both Sexes." He promised that his recovery of the true meaning of Christ's teaching on divorce would "set free many daughters of Israel," as well as give back to man "his just dignity, and prerogative in nature...."[61] At the same time he accepted as axiomatic the Pauline injunction that wives must be subject to their husbands (Colossians 3:18), barring, he noted, the exception that if the wife were wiser, "then a superior and more naturall law comes in, that the wiser should govern the lesse wise, whether male or female." He stressed, however, that the wife's subjection must not be that of a servant, for she was entitled to a large though not equal share in the empire God had given the husband. But having made these qualifications, he went on, in a tone that intimated his own personal grievance, to demand the right of divorce in behalf of the man as the victim of the woman: although created as the inferior sex for the man's good and solace, her "wilfulnes or inability to be a wife frustrates the...end of her creation" and allows the husband to "acquitt himself to freedom by his naturall birthright, and that indelible character of priority which God crown'd him with."[62]

Despite their tangential relationship to politics, Milton's divorce pamphlets harbored the seeds of the concepts on which he was subsequently to rely in his defense of revolution. The principles of which he availed himself in them to set aside the marriage contract were neither philosophically grounded nor systematically developed. Nevertheless, they are conspicuously present as mainstays of his case that the right of divorce when spouses are ill-matched in an unhappy union is a requisite of human liberty and dignity. The critique of custom previously voiced in his tracts against episcopacy here

[60] The role of the principle of Christian liberty in Milton's thought is one of the main themes of Barker's book; for further discussion of this subject, see below, chap. 6. A. S. P. Woodhouse, *Puritanism And Liberty* (London: Dent, 1938), Introduction, pp. [65–68], has stressed the emancipatory potentialities inherent in the concept of Christian liberty when applied to the secular domain during the English revolution.

[61] *The Doctrine And Discipline of Divorce*, p. 355.

[62] *Tetrachordon*, pp. 589–590.

acquired an even sharper tone. In vindication of the novelty of his position he attacked custom as error's ally, each supporting the other in their joint effort to "persecute and chase away all truth and solid wisdome out of humane life...." It is these two and their many vulgar followers who envy and decry "the industry of free reasoning under the terms of humor and innovation, as if the womb of teeming Truth were to be closed up, if shee presume to bring forth ought, that sorts not with their unchewed notions and suppositions."[63] This forthright espousal of free reasoning and unorthodox truth against the power of customary error evinced the increasing separation of the proudly independent author from the mainstream Puritanism of the Presbyterians, his former friends, who found his opinions on marriage scandalous and immoral. It also clearly foreshadowed the issue of unlicensed printing and liberty of the press which was soon to engage his attention. With his writings on divorce, Milton set forth on the road that eventually led him into opposition to every form of orthodoxy as a rebel both in religion and in politics.

Milton intended his work on divorce as a further contribution to the great national reformation which he had fervently looked for ever since the beginning of the Long Parliament. Despite his quarrel with the Presbyterians, his expectations for the renewal of his country under parliament's guidance remained undiminished. In *Areopagitica*, published in November 1644 between the second and third of the divorce pamphlets, he gave the fullest testimonial to the intensity of his political idealism. A plea to parliament in behalf of the liberty of the press, it also touched secondarily on the subject of religious toleration. It is of vital significance among his writings not only for its rhetorical power and the light it sheds on his understanding of liberty, but as a monument to his hopes for the revolution while his faith in its future was still unimpaired.

All the states and churches of early modern Europe took the necessity of press censorship for granted. They all considered the expression of ideas and beliefs far too important for the preservation of political, religious, and social stability to be left unregulated. Well before the era of printing began in England, parliamentary and ecclesiastical legislation in the early fifteenth century instituted a system of censorship and heresy prosecution to suppress the Lollard movement born from the heretical teachings of John Wyclif. Although the Protestant regime established in the sixteenth century by Queen Elizabeth did away with heresy laws, she and her

---

[63] *The Doctrine And Discipline of Divorce*, pp. 223–224.

49

successors continued to control the press as an essential governmental responsibility, using the corporate organization of the book trade and the requirement of licensing and registration before publication among the instrumentalities for this purpose. Under Charles I, the crown's strenuous efforts to silence dissent resulted in the stringent decree of the Court of Star Chamber in 1637 to strengthen the regulation of printing. In 1641, however, parliament abolished the Star Chamber along with the Court of High Commission, another organ of royal censorship, as illegal and tyrannical tribunals. With their demise, the principal weapons for enforcing censorship ceased to be available. Yet it was never parliament's intention to leave the press free and open to the expression of all opinions. Following several preliminary measures, it passed an ordinance in July 1643 to suppress the many false, seditious, and libelous books and pamphlets defamatory of religion and government. Among the several ways to attain this end, it required the licensing and approval of all writings prior to their publication by parliamentary-appointed censors.[64]

This was part of the context of the appearance of *Areopagitica*, which Milton wrote as a protest against the licensing provision of the ordinance. In doing so he was not lacking a personal motive. The criticism of his divorce tracts included calls for their suppression. The first of them, *The Doctrine And Discipline of Divorce*, was not licensed before publication and may perhaps have been denied approval. The second, *The Judgement of Martin Bucer*, was licensed; but in its concluding postscript Milton voiced concern that "in a time of reformation" and "of free speaking, free writing," his work should fail to find "a permission to the Presse." He went on to appeal to wise men "whether truth be suffer'd to be truth, or liberty to be liberty now among us, and be not again in danger of new fetters and captivity...."[65] These words foreshadow the argument of *Areopagitica*, which was published only a few months later. Parliamentary censorship was ineffectual, however, and it is a point of considerable interest that neither *Areopagitica* nor the two subsequent pamphlets on divorce were licensed for publication, probably because they deliberately ignored the licensing requirement.

Apart from the licensing ordinance itself, there was another, much broader context to which *Areopagitica* was related. In the same

---

[64] The text of the licensing ordinance is printed in *Acts And Ordinances of The Interregnum*, ed. C. H. Firth and R. S. Rait, 3 vols. (London: HMSO, 1911), vol. I, pp. 184–187.

[65] *The Judgement of Martin Bucer*, p. 479.

postscript cited above, Milton also warned against an "ecclesiastical thraldom, which under new shapes and disguises begins afresh to grow upon us."[66] This was an allusion to the Presbyterians' attempt to impose their exclusive church discipline on the nation and suppress its opponents. It pointed to the contested question of religious toleration, which became a highly divisive issue among parliament's supporters as the civil war continued. The general desire for reformation which united them in 1640–41 had given way by 1644 to very sharp disagreements as to what its character should be. Most Puritans favored a Presbyterian national establishment to replace episcopacy. Some wanted this church to be autonomous and wholly free from parliamentary control, while others, wary of the danger of clerical domination, held the Erastian view that it must be subject to the ultimate authority of parliament. In the summer of 1643 parliament convened the Westminster Assembly, a body of 120 ministers plus 30 members of the Lords and the Commons and some representatives of the Scottish church, to advise it on reformation. An overwhelming segment of clerical opinion in the assembly desired a Presbyterian form of church government exempt from state control. A small minority of Independents (i.e., Congregationalists) in the assembly, on the other hand, while not opposed to the principle of a national church, refused to consent to a compulsory Presbyterian uniformity and maintained that each parochial congregation should be independent in its discipline and not subordinate to any external ecclesiastical jurisdiction. These Independent ministers sympathized within limits with the demand for toleration by the separatist religious bodies which had been rapidly springing up and rejected any association with a national church.

The differences between Presbyterians and Independents were also increasingly felt in parliament. Although a majority in the House of Commons was willing to accept Presbyterianism subject to parliamentary control, a lesser number consisting of Independents and some others, were averse to a repressive religious uniformity and would have extended toleration to the tender consciences of Protestant dissenters unwilling to join in a national church. The Presbyterians feared and rejected toleration as the parent of heresy, schism, and religious anarchy. Their position was strengthened when parliament in the fall of 1643 made the Solemn League and Covenant with rebel Scotland, a treaty providing for Scottish intervention against the king in the English civil war. The Covenanters were rigid Presbyterians, determined as the price of their assistance to bring the

---

[66] Ibid., p. 479.

English and Scottish churches into the closest conformity with one another. During 1644 the question of religious toleration moved into the forefront of controversy as a topic of heated debate in sermons and the press. A broad–based coalition composed of the Independents and their allies emerged in opposition to the Presbyterians' ambition of fastening their discipline upon the kingdom. From within this camp came a stream of notable pamphlets by authors like Henry Robinson, William Walwyn, John Goodwin, Roger Williams, and others who attacked the Presbyterian's intolerance and defended the right of the separatist sects and peaceable believers to practice their faith free from persecution by state or church. Some of these writers presented the case for toleration with a comprehensiveness of reasons never yet seen in Europe in connection with this subject.[67]

All these developments announced the inexorable disintegration of English Puritanism into irreconcilable antagonistic parties as the war with the king continued. Milton, who had his own dispute with the Presbyterians because of their disapproval of his divorce tracts, registered this division in *Areopagitica*. The latter tract, nevertheless, while indicating its author's belief in toleration, was only indirectly related to this fundamental problem, since its main focus lay on the subsidiary matter of press freedom. Modeled on a classical oration to the Athenian assembly, the Areopagus, it criticized censorship as a discouragement to learning and an obstacle to the pursuit of truth. Milton's purpose was to persuade parliament of the harmfulness, injustice, and inexpediency of mandating the licensing of books prior to publication, as the 1643 ordinance specified. Throughout he seemed to assume that parliament would correct its error once it heard the voice of reason. As in his previous writings, he drew attention to his own qualifications for offering counsel, based on his "naturall endowments" and a life given to study as one "whom God hath fitted for the speciall use of these times with eminent and ample gifts...."[68] His only wish, he stated, was to promote his country's liberty. He traced the practice of licensing and requiring the censor's *imprimatur* to the tyrannous papal and Spanish Inquisition and the Council of Trent, from which, as he claimed, it had been borrowed by persecuting English bishops and then taken up most recently by

[67] W. K. Jordan, *The Development of Religious Toleration*, 4 vols. (Cambridge, Mass.: Harvard University Press, 1932–1940), surveys the tolerationist literature of the earlier 1640s and deals with Milton in vol. IV, pp. 202–236. Sirluck's introduction, chap. II, discusses contemporary writings on toleration in relation to *Areopagitica*, as does Barker, chap. VI.

[68] *Areopagitica*, CPW, vol. II, pp. 489–490, 567.

"some of our Presbyters." At the beginning of the parliament, the Presbyterians, by disregarding prelatical censorship, "first broke the triple ice clung about our hearts, and taught the people to see day." Since then, however, they have become licensers themselves; once almost silenced by the prelates from preaching, they now try to prevent others from reading and would impose a second tyranny on learning, so that "Bishops and Presbyters are the same to us both name and thing." Milton was indignant that "freedom of writing should be restrain'd by a discipline imitated from the Prelats...to shut us up all again into the brest of a licencer...." Having ousted the bishops, the Presbyterians were striving to get into their seats under another name. Seeing that they were so active in suppressing, "it would be no unequall distribution," he suggested, "...to suppresse the suppressors themselves, whom the change of their condition hath puft up, more then their late experience of harder times hath made wise...."[69]

Milton condemned book licensing in the name of both reason and freedom as the foundation of virtue. Those who wished to suppress books pretended that their purpose was to shield people from the contamination of evil. God, however, had entrusted man with the gift of reason, which meant "freedom to choose, for reason is but choosing." Good and evil, moreover, were so intermingled in the world that it was impossible to know and distinguish the one without being exposed to the other. He poured scorn on the notion that virtue lay in ignorance or could be developed under the direction of law and compulsion. True virtue consisted in the capacity to choose the good freely based on the knowledge of evil. The "true warfaring Christian" was one who, knowing vice with all its baits and pleasures, yet preferred what is good. "I cannot praise a fugitive and cloister'd vertue," he said, "unexercis'd & unbreath'd, that never sallies out and sees her adversary, but slinks out of the race where that immortal garland is to be won, not without dust and heat." What purifies individuals "is triall, and triall is by what is contrary." Since the knowledge of vice "is so necessary to the constituting of human vertue, and the scanning of error to the confirmation of truth, how can we," he inquired, "more safely, and with lesse danger, scout into the regions of sin and falsity then by reading all manner of tractates and hearing all manner of reason?"[70]

Areopagitica expressed an intense belief in the ever-increasing revelation of knowledge and truth, and Milton further opposed

---

[69] Ibid., pp. 487, 493, 505, 539, 541, 568–569.
[70] Ibid., pp. 513–514, 515, 516–517, 527.

licensing because it hindered their progress. If they were to grow and reformation advance, people had to be free to publish their thoughts and let them be heard. For himself, he said, "give me the liberty to know, to utter, and to argue freely according to conscience, above all liberties." Like virtue, which must prove itself through encounter with evil, so truth could only be tested in battle with falsehood. Nor did she need a licenser to safeguard her victory; let her grapple with her adversary, he urged, for truth was never "put to the wors, in a free and open encounter."[71]

Liberty and reason are thus indissolubly linked in *Areopagitica* in order to insure the triumph of virtue and truth. Milton, indeed, could never think of any of these as separable from one another. Reason serves the cause of liberty and liberty is necessary to virtue and promotes truth. The moral dimension prevails throughout this argument. The strenuous conception of virtue it entails is altogether characteristic of Milton and forms a cardinal motif of his personal philosophy. From early youth he had prepared himself with the utmost concentration to be a great poet and thinker. Self-mastery as an artist, man, and Christian, the essence of virtue in its contest with temptation and distraction, was a keynote of his character. *Areopagitica* gave fresh expression to this fundamental conviction, which presupposed a nature as strong as his own, distinguished by exceptional independence and self-confidence, envisaging life as a continual challenge to self-conquest.

The intimate connection existing for Milton between liberty and virtue caused him to set definite limits to freedom of the press. Unlike the modern liberal, he could not conceive of freedom as either real or justifiable when exercised contrary to morality and virtue. Recognizing the power of books, he was therefore not opposed to their regulation, and willingly accepted that "it is of greatest concernment in the Church and Commonwealth, to have a vigilant eye how [they] demeane themselves, as well as men; and thereafter to confine, imprison, and do sharpest justice on them as malefactors."[72] Practically speaking, this meant that although against censorship before publication, he did not object to it afterward, if a book proved to be harmful or immoral. He made this point unmistakably clear at the conclusion of *Areopagitica*, when he declared his approval of the burning and destruction of books once published, should they "be found mischievous and libellous...." This method, he claimed, "will be the timeliest and the most effectual remedy, that mans prevention

[71] Ibid., pp. 549–550, 560, 561–563.
[72] Ibid., p. 492.

can use."[73] Following the revolution of 1688 and the establishment of press freedom in the eighteenth century, Milton's view opposing licensing and prior censorship but accepting an author's liability after publication became the prevailing legal doctrine. It was clearly stated in Sir William Blackstone's famous *Commentaries on The Laws of England*, which declared that a free press was essential in a free state and that every freeman had the right to publish what he pleased but must take the consequences if he published dangerous or offensive writings.[74]

Milton's conception of freedom of the press thus included significant qualifications strongly at variance with modern libertarian views of the subject. In taking this position, moreover, he was in no way guilty of contradiction. Greatly as he valued liberty, he never thought of it as an end in itself, and considered it good only if united with virtue.

It is only fair to add, though, that given the balance of its arguments and the context in which it appeared, *Areopagitica* in its general character was predominantly an eloquent plea in favor of liberty in which the qualifications were relatively of little importance. Milton called for liberty at this juncture in behalf of all of parliament's supporters, inspired by his passionate belief in the justice of the parliamentary cause and his confidence in the moral regeneration of the English people. In the great outburst of discussion the revolution provoked, he saw proof that his country-men had become a community of truth-seekers. He proudly reminded parliament of the great nation it governed, of its keen intelligence and piercing spirit, "acute to invent, suttle and sinewy to discours, not beneath the reach of any point the highest that human capacity can soar to." He knew that God is beginning "some new and great period in the Church," and has revealed himself first "as his manner is...to his English men." This was an old theme of English

---

[73] Ibid., p. 569. Milton's restrictions on freedom of the press, as well as those on religious toleration which are noted further on in my discussion, constitute the main thesis of John Illo's "The Misreading of Milton," first published in the *Columbia Journalism Review* and reprinted in *Radical Perspectives in The Arts*, ed. Lee Baxandall (Harmondsworth: Penguin, 1972). Illo berates Milton scholarship and the poet's admirers for failing to see that *Areopagitica* is neither liberal nor libertarian. Although he is right to describe it as a militant and exclusivist revolutionary pamphlet, he entirely overlooks the fact that the spirit of the work and certain of its arguments are capable of transcending the limits Milton himself placed on liberty of the press and religion.

[74] Blackstone's *Commentaries*, 4 vols. (Oxford, 1765–69), vol 4. pp. 151–152, cited by John Phillip Reid, *The Concept of Liberty in The Age of The American Revolution* (Chicago: University of Chicago Press, 1988), p. 118.

Protestantism which Milton raised to an apocalyptic pitch. His vision opened out further to embrace the vast city of London, a Parliamentarian stronghold, "the mansion house of liberty" and a shop of war where "armed Justice" defends "beleaguer'd Truth" while many minds eagerly search out new ideas in homage to the approaching reformation and, reading and testing all things, assent to "the force of reason and convincement." His country, he exulted, had cast off the old skin of corruption and become young again, entering "the glorious waies of Truth and prosperous vertue...." In yet another image of renewal, he pictured his people as "a noble and puissant nation" arising like a strong man after sleep and, like an eagle, mewing its invincible youth as it gazed with undazzled eyes at the full noonday beam.[75] To parliament he voiced his gratitude for its "faithful guidance," "undaunted Wisdome," and "indefatigable vertues." He told the Lords and Commons that their "mild, and free, and human government" was the cause of "all this free writing and free speaking." He extolled them for their "valorous and happy counsels," which "have purchast us liberty, the nurse of all great wits." And he admonished them that they "cannot make us now lesse capable, lesse knowing, and lesse eagerly pursuing of the truth," unless they first themselves became oppressive and arbitrary, which they could not be.[76]

In this intensely idealistic frame of mind he also urged toleration for the sects, whose spread many Puritans found so alarming. Throughout his discussion, though, he never identified himself with the sects in any way; while regarding them sympathetically, it was always from a distance, without ever noticing any of them individually. Certain that new religious knowledge remained to be discovered, he attacked the Presbyterians, who perpetually complain of sects and "make it such a calamity that any man dissents from their maxims." He blamed their own pride and ignorance as the cause of disturbance, because instead of hearing reason and trying to convince, they wish to suppress those who disagree. Scoffing at the "fantastic terrors of sect and schism," he saw the sects as a sign of "the earnest and zealous thirst after knowledge and understanding which God hath stirr'd up in this City." His call was for charity and forbearance in a fraternal search for truth, and for renouncing "this Prelaticall tradition of crowding free consciences and Christian liberties into canons and precepts of men." Differences were inevitable, he held, in building the temple of the Lord, whose

[75] *Areopagitica*, pp. 551, 553–554, 557–558.
[76] Ibid., p. 487, 559.

symmetry and perfection would consist in a harmony of "many moderat varieties and brotherly dissimilitudes that are not vastly disproportionate...."[77]

In *Areopagitica*, Milton did not explore the problem of toleration sufficiently to discuss the power the magistrate or civil authority ought to possess in religion. He left aside the question of the relationship between church and state, even though this was a crucial aspect of the subject which a number of other writers examined.[78] His endorsement of toleration rested on an understanding of liberty that allowed for the coexistence of many religious societies provided they were in accord on the fundamentals of faith. While not attempting to define these fundamentals, he held that, aside from them, Christianity left many things indifferent in religion in which individuals should be free to believe or not as reason and conscience directed.[79] "...if all cannot be of one mind," he observed, "as who looks they should? this doubtles is more wholsome, more prudent, and more Christian that many be tolerated rather then all compell'd." He immediately added, nevertheless, that such liberty could not extend to "Popery, and open superstition" nor to what is "impious or evil...or absolutely...against faith or manners." The tolerance he commended encompassed only "those neighboring differences, or rather indifferences...whether on some point of doctrine or of discipline....which though they be many, yet need not interrupt the unity of spirit, if we could find among us the bond of peace." This standard most evidently excluded Catholicism because, according to Milton, it "extirpats all religions and civill supremacies" and should therefore itself be extirpated.[80] It would likewise have excluded those antinomian sects whose members considered themselves emancipated

---

[77] Ibid., pp. 550, 554, 555.

[78] Sirluck, pp. 169–170, 176, makes heavy weather of Milton's failure to argue for the separation of church and state in *Areopagitica*, contending that this omission was part of a deliberate strategy to win support for his opposition to licensing from the Erastians in parliament, who would never have countenanced such a separation. Nigel Smith, "*Areopagitica*: Voicing Contexts 1643–5," in *Politics, Poetics And Hermeneutics in Milton's Prose*, ed. David Loewenstein and James G. Turner (Cambridge: Cambridge University Press, 1990), pp. 194–196, adopts Sirluck's opinion that *Areopagitica* was a calculated appeal to the Erastians. This explanation of Milton's position invents a false problem, and is needless as well as devoid of evidence. *Areopagitica* was mainly concerned with press licensing, not toleration. In all likelihood, at the time he wrote it Milton had not yet thought through the problem of the magistrate's power in religion, although at a later date he was to hold that the church must be separate from the state.

[79] See Barker's comments, pp. 96–97, 361n.92.

[80] *Areopagitica*, p. 565.

from obedience to the moral law by their interior possession of the spirit. The episcopal church also, even if placed on a voluntary basis, would probably have had no claim to toleration in Milton's eyes.

In these restrictions on religious liberty, he again prescribed a boundary in accord with his fundamental moral outlook. In essence, it solicited liberty exclusively for those who merited it, the Puritan denominations and sectarian congregations comprised within the spectrum of parliament's adherents. For Catholicism in particular he adamantly refused, as did most Protestants, to recognize any right of conscience. From his Italian journey he recalled his meeting with the famous Galileo, imprisoned by the Inquisition "for thinking in Astronomy otherwise then the Franciscan and Dominican licensers thought."[81] He regarded Catholicism as a persecuting, idolatrous superstition whose theocratic claims and papal supremacy made it an enemy of the civil power and true religion undeserving of tolerance.

Although *Areopagitica* is the most famous of Milton's prose writings, the only one still recommended to general readers and uncritically celebrated since the later nineteenth century as a deathless plea for liberty of the press and thought, its contemporary impact was negligible. It made no noticeable difference to the licensing controversy. In the wide-ranging debate on religious toleration, it was also barely taken into account and overshadowed by the writings of other advocates of liberty of conscience whose views were broader than his own.

Milton's aspirations to fame and a prophetic public role in serving his country led him to take an early part in the controversies of the English revolution. Whether he was writing about episcopacy, divorce, or press licensing, he did so in the consciousness of possessing extraordinary gifts which peculiarly fitted him to deal with these subjects as an adviser. Three of his four divorce pamphlets were addressed to parliament and the first of them to the Westminster Assembly as well. *Areopagitica* too was directed to parliament. He intended all of these works as a contribution to the reformation he eagerly awaited. Save for the censures his divorce tracts aroused, however, they made little impression at the time. They failed to bring him the renown he sought or to gain him stature as one whose writings could shape the course of public discussion. Very evident in these compositions of the earlier 1640s was the apocalyptic strain the revolution inspired in him and his wholehearted commitment to its cause. His resentment of the Presbyterians' intolerance did not shake his belief in the English

---

[81] Ibid., p. 538.

people, who at this juncture received his glowing approbation as he hailed their awakening so fervently in *Areopagitica*. The liberty he advocated in the latter was a qualified liberty; it was reserved for spiritual aristocrats like himself and for those he considered servants and followers of truth and virtue. He put this thought once more into a sonnet of 1646 against the detractors of his divorce tracts, in which he distinguished liberty from license and pronounced that those who loved liberty "must first be wise and good."[82] The rest, who failed to meet this criterion, had no right to liberty. As internal divisions multiplied with the revolution's advance, he was to consign more and more of its earlier supporters to this category.

[82] *Sonnet XII*, "On The Detraction Which Followed upon My Writing Certain Treatises," CF, p. 295.

Chapter 3

MILTON IN REVOLUTION:
REGICIDE AND THE RIGHT OF REVOLUTION

After finishing the last of his divorce tracts, Milton refrained from further pamphleteering and controversy for the next four years. His life during this time underwent considerable alteration. In 1645 his wife returned, pleading for his forgiveness and asking to be reunited. He took her back, "his own generous nature," said Edward Phillips, being "more inclinable to Reconciliation than to perseverance in Anger and Revenge."[1]. Although it is hard to believe that he felt the same passion and affection for her as before, and one wonders too what she made of his writings on divorce, they apparently remained in harmony until her death in 1652.[2] In the autumn he left Aldersgate Street for a larger house in the Barbican, which his aged father and several of his pupils also shared with him. Within a year his wife bore their first child, a girl. Two other girls and a boy who died in infancy were subsequently born to them. Mary Milton's parents with their five younger children were staying in Oxford, the king's head-quarters, when it surrendered in June 1646 to the victorious parliamentary army as the civil war came to an end. Its property sequestered by the parliamentary forces, the Powell family took refuge in Milton's house in London, allowing him no peace to study or work. At the close of the year Powell died, leaving an encumbered estate and still in debt to his son-in-law for the old loan as well as his daughter's unpaid dowry. The elder Milton died three months later. In a letter to a Florentine friend from the halcyon days of his Italian journey, Milton described his unhappy state of mind, lamenting that he was compelled by law and accident to be with people with whom he had nothing in common and whose presence exhausted him. "I

---

[1] Edward Phillips, *The Life of Mr. John Milton*, in *The Early Lives of Milton*, ed. Helen Darbishire (London: Constable, 1932), p. 67.
[2] See the comments of both John and Edward Phillips, ibid., pp. 31, 67.

am forced to live," he complained, "in almost perpetual solitude."[3] Finally, to his relief, Mrs. Powell and her children departed, and in the late summer of 1647 he moved again to a smaller house in High Holborn where he seems to have been able to resume a less troubled existence. By this time, though, he was experiencing considerable difficulty with his eyesight and beginning to fear the possibility of blindness.

By the mid–1640s Milton was probably reasonably well known as a learned man and author on a number of different subjects. In 1643, the year in which Samuel Hartlib, one of the most active educational and social reformers of the revolutionary era, probably first made his acquaintance, he observed that Milton had written many good books and was full of projects and ideas.[4] Knowing that he kept a school, Hartlib urged him to put down his thoughts on the reform of education. Despite his preoccupation with his divorce tracts, he complied in a short treatise, *Of Education*, which either he or Hartlib arranged to have published in June 1644. His scheme of schooling disdained all utilitarian objects, being designed as a liberal education for boys during the years from twelve to twenty-one which would supply the place equally of school and university. It was highly impractical not only in this respect but in its very taxing curriculum. Its interest from a political standpoint lies in the way it retains the consistently aristocratic assumptions that informed his thinking. The training he envisaged was not intended for the common people nor for "any yeoman or tradesman," but for "noble and gentle youth." This aim was similarly reflected in his definition of "a compleate and generous Education" (and we should recall that the contemporary meaning of "generous" signified good birth and breeding) as one "which fits a man to perform justly, skilfully and magnanimously all the offices both private and publike of peace and war."[5] Milton's educational idealism was thus centered on the moral and intellectual formation of a governing elite of aristocratic character, combining both virtue and knowledge, such as he had earlier imagined in *Comus*.

Apart from the fact that he wrote little verse during the 1640s, until 1645 little of his earlier poetry had been printed. In October of the latter year, doubtless to make himself better known as a poet, he published a collection of his poems in English, Latin, and Greek. A principal feature of this edition was the general impression it

---

[3] Letter of 21 April 1647 to Carlo Dati, CPW, vol. II, pp. 762–763.
[4] G. H. Turnbull, *Hartlib, Dury And Comenius* (London: Liverpool University Press, 1947), pp. 39–40.
[5] *Of Education*, 1644, CPW, vol. II, pp. 370, 377–379, 406.

contrived to give of ignoring or transcending the bitter divisions of civil war in which it appeared. The title page announced that the songs were set to music by "Mr. Henry Lawes Gentleman of the Kings Chappel, and one of His Majesties Musick." The prefatory encomium by the publisher, Humphrey Moseley, a man of Royalist sympathies, associated the author's work with the recently published "choice peeces" of the poet Edmund Waller, whom parliament had banished for complicity in a Royalist plot. The volume included early elegies on a couple of bishops, an epitaph on a Catholic noblewoman, the marchioness of Winchester, and Latin poems addressed to several of Milton's Italian friends who were likewise Catholics. It also contained tributes to the poet from the latter and from Sir Henry Wotton, a courtier, ambassador, and man of letters now deceased. Preceding the text of *Comus*, which was reproduced from the 1637 edition, was Henry Lawes' dedication of the poem to Viscount Brackley, heir to the earl of Bridgewater, in whose honor the masque was written. In 1645 both the earl and his son were Royalists. The sole clue to the author's political attitude was the new headnote appended to *Lycidas* stating that the poem "foretels the ruine of our corrupted Clergy than in their height." Notwithstanding Milton's intense personal belief in the Parliamentarian side in the civil war, it was as if he wished in this collection to present a different aspect of himself, that of a gentleman, scholar, and poet whose dedication to the eternal values of art soared far above local conflicts and division.[6]

When Milton became involved once more in controversy in 1649, much had happened to change the political scene in the intervening four years. Parliament's military victory failed to bring any kind of settlement and the Parliamentarian coalition was irreparably shattered into contending parties. Widespread popular discontent and disaffection existed due to economic hardship, the severe losses

---

[6] I have used this edition in the facsimile, *Poems of Mr. John Milton* (Menston: Scolar Press, 1970); see the discussion of its features by Louis Martz, *Poet of Exile* (New Haven: Yale University Press, 1980), chap. 2, and Parker's remarks, vol. I, p. 288. For Humphrey Moseley's Royalism and support of Royalist authors, see P. W. Thomas, *Sir John Berkenhead 1617–1679. A Royalist Career in Politics And Polemics* (Oxford: Clarendon Press, 1969), pp. 134, 144. The 1645 edition of Milton's poems has even been seen as the product of a quest for respectability in which he sought to distance himself from the religious sectarians and lower-class people on the Parliamentarian side; Thomas N. Corns, "Milton's Quest for Respectability," *Modern Language Review*, vol. 77, no. 4 (1982). Annabel Patterson, " 'Forc'd Fingers': Milton's Early Poems And Ideological Constraints," in *"The Muses Common-Weale." Poetry And Politics in The Seventeenth Century*, ed. Claude J. Summers and Ted-Larry Pebworth (Columbia: University of Missouri Press, 1988), considers it one of the evidences of Milton's ideological contradictions which his masterly self-construction has concealed from modern readers.

inflicted by the war, and the heavy burden of parliamentary taxation. In 1646 parliament had voted to abolish bishops and establish a Presbyterian national church subject to its own control, thus worsening the split between Presbyterians and Independents and leading the former to seek the king's support for their ecclesiastical system in return for concessions to him. Despite his military defeat Charles I's concurrence in a future settlement still seemed indispensable to political men, and he strove to exploit the differences among his adversaries to recover some of his power. In the parliamentary army, Independency and sectarianism had gained many converts among both officers and common soldiers, including its lieutenant general and most successful commander, Oliver Cromwell. A new radical movement had also sprung up, the Levellers, with adherents in the London populace and the army, which agitated for liberty of conscience and democratic political change, not least the reform of parliament itself. In June 1647, after parliament dominated by its Presbyterian majority voted to disband the army, the latter refused to obey in a common front of officers and men. Driven by their grievances, which included arrears in pay and other complaints, the defiant soldiers rapidly became politicized under Independent and Leveller influence. Convinced that they had fought the civil war for religious and political liberty, they feared that the Presbyterians would join with the king to reinstate him on terms that betrayed the cause for which the war was waged. Meanwhile, although the Scottish army had returned home after parliament's victory, the Scottish leaders, who continued to press for a common church order in the two countries, contemplated intervening in England once again, this time in support of the Presbyterians and the king.

In the complex maneuvers with Charles I that followed on the part of the Presbyterians, Independents, and the Scots, he finally made a secret treaty with the Scots providing for a Scottish invasion to reestablish his rights in return for his acceptance of the Presbyterian system for three years. This alliance set the stage for a second civil war in 1648. Amidst the outbreak of scattered Royalist risings that were presently crushed, the Scots entered England in force in the summer, only to be destroyed by Cromwell's army at Preston. In the aftermath of their victory, the army's leaders resolved to put an end to the English Presbyterians' dealings with the king and to punish the latter for his crimes. In December 1648 the army forcibly expelled nearly one hundred members from the House of Commons, leaving a minority which would support its measures. The purged House, which became known as the Rump, then voted on 1 January 1649 to appoint a high court of justice to try the king. A few days later it resolved that the people were, under God, the source of all just power, and that the Commons, being elected by the people, formed the supreme power in England without the concurrence of the king or House of Lords. With this revolutionary decision, which was subsequently ratified in formal acts abolishing the monarchy and House of Lords, the truncated House of Commons assumed the sovereign authority of parliament to itself alone and made the English state a commonwealth or republic. Later in that same month Charles I was brought to trial, charged with betraying his trust to rule according to law for the people's good. Despite his refusal to acknowledge the court's jurisdiction, he was pronounced guilty and sentenced to die. On 30 January he was beheaded in front of Whitehall Palace before a huge crowd.

These events produced a shock throughout the country and abroad. The general opinion looked with horror on the king's execution as a criminal act of sacrilege. Many of parliament's former supporters turned against it. The members secluded from the House of Commons condemned the army and the Rump for their lawless actions. Beside the enmity of the defeated Royalists, the new regime had to contend with the hostility of the Presbyterians, who loudly denounced the king's trial and death in sermons and pamphlets as sinful and illegal. The Levellers also attacked the new government as a self-appointed, self-perpetuating oligarchy devoid of authority. Even before the army's purge, the Long Parliament, already sitting for eight long years, had ceased in any real sense to represent the country. After the purge, the Rump had even less claim to speak as the nation's representative body. Although professing to derive its power from the people, it enjoyed only a narrow basis of support and depended entirely on the army for its survival. If a free parliamentary election had been held after 1649, it would have led in all probability to the prompt restoration of the Stuart monarchy. The blatant contradiction between the commonwealth's claim to rule as an organ of popular sovereignty and its actual position as an unrepresentative minority regime was something from which it was never able to escape.

The principal agents responsible for the commonwealth's existence were the leading Independents in the army and the House of Commons, foremost among them Oliver Cromwell. Like Cromwell, most were Puritan gentlemen belonging to the traditional landed governing class. They believed strongly in liberty of conscience and parliamentary supremacy in the name of the people, and were determined to prevent the gains of the civil war from being sacrificed to the repressive intolerance of the Presbyterians or the needs of a compromise with the king. With very few exceptions they were pragmatists, not doctrinaire republicans. Had it been possible for them to achieve an agreement with Charles I, they would have been willing to accept a limited kingship guaranteed by various political securities along with provisions for the toleration of religious dissent. When they put Charles I to death, abolished the monarchy, and made England a republic governed by a single-chamber parliament, they were convinced that they acted from unavoidable necessity because their adversaries had left them no other choice. Some were equally certain that in doing these things, as in their military victories over the Royalists and the Scots, they were God's chosen instruments guided by providence.[7]

It was with this regime and its leadership that Milton most closely identified himself. Fundamentally, his sympathies lay with the Independents, whose political actions he approved and was prepared to defend in detail. In February 1649 he published *The Tenure of Kings And Magistrates*, a justification of regicide and the people's right to revolt and remove their rulers who become tyrants. This tract, reprinted in a larger edition in 1650, was his first devoted entirely to politics and political theory. It was a short work, not exceeding sixty pages in its enlarged version. Although in a sense a *pièce d'occasion*, it nevertheless contained the basic political convictions at which he had arrived through his experience of revolution.

By the time he wrote it his mood was far different than four years before. The apocalyptic strain had vanished. His hope of a great reformation had waned, and he no longer felt his former faith in the wisdom and loyalty of the English people. The disunity that had befallen the Parliamentarian cause, the losses and corruption incident to the war, political confusion and the failure to attain a settlement resulting in a second civil war, finally, popular and Presbyterian opposition to the newly established commonwealth, all contributed to a growing disillusionment. Its signs are clearly discernible in several of his works of the late 1640s. A rendering of nine psalms into English verse made in April 1648 seems, as his biographer suggests, to be the product of a "troubled and despairing soul".[8] Altogether, the psalms Milton selected imply, in their image of Israel, an England that has turned away from God and forfeited his favor.

[7] David Underdown, *Pride's Purge* (Oxford: Clarendon Press, 1971), and Blair Worden, *The Rump Parliament* (Cambridge: Cambridge University Press, 1974), Introduction and pts. 1–3, describe the developments leading up to the king's execution and the creation of the commonwealth.

[8] Parker, vol. I, p. 322.

They implore God to withdraw his anger from his people and grant them his mercy. The last of them, a personal outcry to God for help in the face of besetting darkness, may also reflect the poet's fear of approaching blindness.[9]

A related note is struck in a sonnet in praise of the parliamentary army's commander-in-chief, Sir Thomas Fairfax, written in August 1648 at the time of the second civil war. It offers a bleak picture of England's condition:

> For what can war, but endless war still breed,
> Till truth and right from violence be freed,
> And public faith cleared from the shameful brand
> Of public fraud. In vain doth valour bleed
> While avarice, and rapine share the land.[10]

Evidence of disenchantment is equally present in *The History of Britain*, of which nearly all of the first four books were written between 1646 and 1649. If we could accept that the so-called *Digression* on the character of the Long Parliament in the third book, which Milton suppressed in the *History's* publication in 1670 and was first printed only posthumously in 1681, belongs to the year 1648 or 1649, then his disillusion would already have been complete. This *Digression*, a far-fetched comparison between fifth and seventeenth-century England, is a severe condemnation of the oppression, corruption, and utter failure of the Long Parliament to live up to its promise. I agree, however, with Professor Woolrych's judgment that it was most likely written in 1660 and hence expresses the author's feelings at the advent of the Restoration.[11] Even so, the passages of earlier date in *The History of Britain* indicate that his attitude to his country had soured. Thus, in another implied parallel, he spoke of the "confused Anarchy" of his time and reprehended his nation for lacking "the wisdom, the virtue" to "govern well themselves" or "use and maintain true libertie...." And of the Britons he noted that

---

[9] Milton's translations are those of Psalms 80 to 88, printed in CF, pp. 308–321; see Parker's comments, vol. I, pp. 322–324.

[10] "On The Lord General Fairfax at The Siege of Colchester," CF, pp. 322–323.

[11] *The History of Britain* and *Digression, Mr. John Miltons Character of The Long Parliament*, are printed in CPW, vol. V, pt. I. The editor, French Fogle, discusses their character and probable dates in his introduction to each. In disagreement with his conclusion that the *Digression* was composed in the spring of 1648 (p. 433), Austin Woolrych argues convincingly for 1660; see his "The Date of The Digression in Milton's *History of Britain*," in *For Veronica Wedgwood These. Studies in Seventeenth-Century History*, ed. Richard Ollard and Pamela Tudor-Craig (London: Collins, 1986).

they were "weak and shallow" in "matters of Government and search of truth...."[12]

The Tenure of Kings And Magistrates was written during Charles I's trial and probably completed just after his execution.[13] Its style offers further evidence of Milton's changed mood. It is much less rhetorical and more austere than his preceding works. Its imagery is sparser and less rich and its logic clearer. Generally, it leaves no doubt that the author's state of mind had become much more sober. He had retrenched his earlier hopes, and those that remained were now all invested in the new republican order. As a contribution to political theory, the *Tenure* was not distinguished by any originality. The substance of its ideas derived from well known classical and sixteenth-century sources justifying resistance to tyrants, and from some of the recent public declarations of the army and parliament against the king. The *Remonstrance* of the officers of the army, issued in November 1648, in which they asserted the sovereignty of the people and announced their intention to proceed judicially against Charles I; the charge on which the king was tried; and the speech that the commonwealth's solicitor, John Cook, had prepared to deliver if the king had pleaded to the charge instead of denying the court's jurisdiction, all contained conceptions similar to Milton's.[14]

Although written, as Milton later said, to reconcile the people's minds to the king's removal,[15] the *Tenure* was not primarily directed at the Royalists; its main target was the Presbyterians, parliament's one-time allies who now fiercely attacked the army and Charles I's deposition. What specifically elicited it, as Milton also explained, were the condemnations of the army's actions by Presbyterian ministers.[16] A typical broadside was fired by forty-seven Presbyterian clergy in and around London on the eve of the king's trial. They

---

[12] *The History of Britain*, pp. 129, 131, 139–140.

[13] *The Tenure of Kings And Magistrates* is printed from the 1650 edition in CPW, vol. III, with an introduction to the volume by Merritt Y. Hughes which sets the work in its context of contemporary argument; see his discussion of the *Tenure's* date of composition, pp. 101–106.

[14] *A Remonstrance of His Excellency...Lord Fairfax...And of The Generall Councell of Officers* (London, 1648); the charge against the king is printed in S. R. Gardiner, *The Constitutional Documents of The Puritan Revolution 1625–1660* (Oxford: Clarendon Press, 1936, pp. 371–374; John Cook, *King Charls His Case* (London, 1649). Perez Zagorin, *A History of Political Thought in The English Revolution* (London: Routledge & Kegan Paul, 1954), chap. VI, discusses the work of John Goodwin and other publicists who wrote in behalf of the commonwealth to defend the execution of Charles I and the people's right to change their governors.

[15] *A Second Defence of The English People*, 1654, CPW, vol. IV, pt. I, p. 627.

[16] Ibid., p. 626.

accused the army of breaking parliament's former pledges and of overthrowing "the whole frame and...Constitution of the Kingdome" by its purge of the Commons and its divesting the king of his authority and using violence against his person. Denying that the army's successes signified the approval of providence, they warned that "it is one of the greatest Judgements, when God suffers men to prosper in sinfull courses." They refused to accept the plea of necessity as an excuse for the army's proceedings; such a necessity, they asserted, "must be Absolute, Present, and Clear; not Doubtful, Uncertain, and Conjectural, as that...alledged in your case must be, being discerned onely by your selves and your own party." The authors' conclusion foretold God's punishment on the army and its partisans unless they turned from their evil ways.[17] Milton was incensed by these statements, which he viewed as the rankest hypocrisy, since the Presbyterians had previously authorized the taking of arms against the king in the civil war. To confute them was one of the principal motives of his defense of regicide.

If this defense was lacking in originality, it was nonetheless one of the first publications to speak out in support of the trial and execution of the king, and was thus of considerable import as a political affirmation, given the context of its appearance. Kings had often been deposed and killed in Europe's past; in England prior to the time of Charles I, five monarchs – Edward II, Richard II, Henry VI, Edward V, and Richard III – lost their thrones through rebellion or usurpation. In the case of Richard II, his removal in 1399 was solemnly ratified in a constitutional process by an assembly of the estates of the realm which declared him worthy of being deprived for many crimes. On the continent, the Act of Abjuration of the States General of the United Netherlands in 1581 formally declared Philip II's forfeiture of his sovereignty for attempting to establish a tyranny over the provinces. Despite such examples, the deposition of Charles I in 1649 was an occurrence without precedent in European history. It was the first time that an anointed king had been placed on trial by a court of his own subjects and sentenced to death for betraying his trust to the people. This act was unique as a proclamation of the principle of popular sovereignty and ruler accountability. If any single event could be said to symbolize the significance of the English revolution in the same way that the Declaration of Independence and the fall of the Bastille did the eighteenth-century revolutions in

[17] *A Serious And Faithfull Representation of The Judgements of Ministers of The Gospell within The Province of London* (London, 1649), pp. 7, 14, 16, 17.

America and France, it was the public execution of Charles I on 30 January 1649.

Milton fully realized the magnitude and unparalleled character of the drama he undertook to justify in the *Tenure*. He spoke contemptuously of those who "swerve, and almost shiver at the Majesty and grandeur" of "the noble Deed" that had been performed. Echoes of the heroism of antiquity appear in his description of those who deposed the king as deliverers of their country "endu'd with fortitude and Heroick vertue...." Although perhaps till now, he said,

> no protestant State or kingdom can be alleg'd to have op'nly put to death thir King, which lately some have writt'n, and imputed to thir great glory; much mistaking the matter. It was not, neither ought to be the glory of a Protestant State, never to have put thir King to death; It is the glory of a Protestant King never to have deserv'd death. And if the Parlament and Military Councel doe what they doe without precedent, if it appear thir duty, it argues the more wisdom, vertue and magnanimity, that they know themselves able to be a precedent to others. Who perhaps in future ages, if they prove not too degenerat, will look up with honour, and aspire to toward these exemplary, and matchless deeds of thir Ancestors, as to the highest top of thir civil glory and emulation.[18]

Milton based his regicide doctrine mainly on the principles of reason and natural right. He posited it as an obvious truth that "all men naturally were borne free" and that after wrong and violence came into the world through Adam's fall, they created kings and magistrates to maintain peace and order subject to covenants and limitations that precluded arbitrary power. Authorities were thus appointed not as the people's lords and masters, but as "thir Deputies and Commissioners" with an "intrusted power." This was the sole imaginable reason why "among free Persons, one man by civil right should beare autority and jurisdiction over another...."[19] From these propositions he deduced a number of conclusions. First, the power of kings and magistrates was derivative and a trust which the people conveyed and which still remained fundamentally in them and could not be taken away without violating "thir natural birthright...." Second, a king guilty of crimes against his people justly forfeits his power, since he exists for their common good. Third, to hold that kings are answerable only to God for their actions would overturn all law and government, render all their oaths and covenants vain, and

[18] *The Tenure of Kings And Magistrates*, pp. 191, 194, 237–238.
[19] Ibid., pp. 198, 199.

lead to the "worst sort of Tyranny" not to be "endur'd by free born men." Finally, since the king or magistrate receives his power "originaly and naturally" from the people for their good, the latter "as oft as they judge it for the best" may either retain or depose him even if not a tyrant, "meerly by the liberty and right of free born Men, to be governed as seems to them best." Further on, he thrust home the same point with specific reference to England. Those who boast, he said,

> as we doe, to be a free Nation, and have not in themselves the power to remove, or to abolish any governour supreme or subordinat, with the government it self upon urgent causes, may please thir fancy with a ridiculous and painted freedom fit to coz'n babies; but are indeed under tyranny and servitude; as wanting that power, which is the root and sourse of all liberty, to dispose and oeconomize in the Land which God hath giv'n them, as Maisters of Family in thir own house and free inheritance.[20]

This was the theoretical essence of Milton's position as a political revolutionary and republican. Adumbrated earlier in his divorce tracts, where the liberty and good of man became the dominant justification for dissolving the marriage bond, it was fundamentally rationalistic in its reliance on presuppositions of natural right, original freedom, popular sovereignty, and contract and corporate consent as the origin of government. By the same right that made the people free to change their governors and government, they were also enabled to overthrow tyrants. Milton defined the tyrant in traditional terms as one who used his power solely in the interests of himself and his faction, heeding neither the law nor common good. Against such a ruler, "the very principles of nature" demonstrated that the people might proceed as they would against a common pest and destroyer of mankind. Although he never once referred to Charles I by name, he left no doubt of the doctrine's application to the king's case. The people of England, he boldly asserted, could lawfully put their king to death for tyranny – a king bound by his covenants to their welfare, who nevertheless treated all laws and parliaments with contempt, held himself unaccountable, and bore the guilt for the destruction of many thousands of his Christian subjects in a civil war.[21]

To buttress these claims, Milton adduced numerous scriptural and historical examples, as well as the opinions of earlier Protestant

[20] Ibid., pp. 202, 203–204, 206, 237.
[21] Ibid., pp. 212, 214.

reformers, both continental and English, who wrote in favor of the right of resistance to ungodly rulers.[22] Among scriptural passages he included Paul's famous injunctions in Romans 13, the *locus classicus* in the New Testament on the duty of obedience, a text he interpreted to prove that subjects were not obliged to obey wicked magistrates.[23] He also drew on English, Scottish, and European history for various instances of the deposition of rulers guilty of tyranny. Among the latter, he stressed particularly the precedents for rebellion afforded by sixteenth-century German Protestants and Scottish Presbyterians.[24] All these arguments, though, were ancillary to the fundamental theoretical conceptions which underlay his case and were mainly intended to counter the charges of the Presbyterian clergy against the army's and parliament's treatment of the king. Milton manifested a bitter dislike of the Presbyterians. Again and again he accused them of falsity to their own principles, sardonically reminding them that they had once cursed the king from their pulpits and incited resistance to him as a tyrant, yet now called him a lawful magistrate and the Lord's anointed immune from punishment.[25] He criticized them for whipping up popular feeling against the new government and stigmatized their intolerance, their mercenary greed for tithes and benefices, and their pride and ambition for power over the laity.[26]

He made little effort in the *Tenure* to reconcile his affirmation of popular sovereignty with the fact that the commonwealth was the creation of a small unrepresentative minority. All he said on this score was that the determination of who was a tyrant must be left to "the uprighter sort" of magistrates and the part of the people "though in number less by many, in whom faction least hath prevaild above the Law of nature and right reason...."[27] Implicit in this statement was the moral criterion of virtue which he had always considered the condition of entitlement to liberty. "...none can love freedom heartilie but good men," he wrote in the *Tenure*'s opening page; the rest "love not freedom, but licence" and easily give themselves up to tyranny.[28] By means of this basic article of his political creed he could easily rationalize the actual situation in which

---

[22] Among those he cited were Luther, Zwingli, Calvin, Bucer, and the English Puritans Anthony Gilby and Chistopher Goodman; ibid., pp. 243–251; the passage he attributed to Gilby was actually written by John Ponet.

[23] Ibid., pp. 209–210.

[24] Ibid., pp. 219–227.

[25] Ibid., pp. 196–197, 234–235.

[26] Ibid., pp. 196, 236, 239, 241.

[27] Ibid., p. 197.

[28] Ibid., p. 190.

the commonwealth found itself. He could also regard the latter's existence as the just dispensation of providence. "...God and a good cause" had given the army and the Rump their victory; "...Justice and Victory" were "the only warrants through all ages, next under immediat Revelation, to exercise supreame power...."[29] He lauded the new regime for "calling us to liberty and the flourishing deeds of a reformd Common-wealth" and hoped God would "bless us, and be propitious to us who reject a King, to make him onely our leader and supreme governour" in a resemblance to the ancient common-wealth of Israel.[30]

Such were the thoughts with which Milton launched himself as an apologist for the English republic. He did so for no other reason than his genuine belief in the righteousness of its cause. The *Tenure*'s arguments and early appearance apparently made an impression in certain quarters, for a month after its publication, the Council of State, the new government's executive organ, appointed him as its Secretary for Foreign Tongues at a salary of £288 per annum supplemented later by an official lodging. This was his first public recognition. As secretary he performed various functions, the most important being to translate the Council of State's communications to foreign governments into Latin and to write on occasion in behalf of the commonwealth against its enemies. A few days after his appointment the Council asked him to frame a reply to a pamphlet attacking the new government by the Leveller leader, John Lilburne. The Levellers, a democratic opposition, stood for the reform of the political order as outlined in their *Agreement of The People*, a draft constitution envisaging much greater liberty and individual rights than England's republican rulers were ever willing to concede. Strongly opposed to the commonwealth, they warned that it threatened to become a new tyranny, complained of the many grievances still oppressing the people, and demanded a new parliament elected on a far broader suffrage to represent the people.[31] Although for reasons unknown Milton made no answer to this tract, this fact should not be taken to indicate that he may have been in

---

[29] Ibid., pp. 192, 194.

[30] Ibid., p. 236.

[31] The pamphlet was *Englands New Chaines Discovered*, which appeared in two parts in February and March 1649; the second installment was called *The Second Part of Englands New-Chaines Discovered*; see Zagorin, chaps. II–III, and Joseph Frank, *The Levellers* (Cambridge, Mass.: Harvard University Press, 1955), for a discussion of Lilburne's and the Levellers' political ideas and program.

sympathy with the Levellers' views.[32] Nowhere in his writings did he so much as mention the Levellers. Even more to the point, essential differences separated him from them, as his readiness to serve the commonwealth proves. While both shared an allegiance to the principle of popular sovereignty, they gave it a far more radical interpretation than he ever did in their insistence on equal citizenship, individual consent to government, and the reform of the franchise and parliament. Although a republican, he was never a democrat, and the qualification of reason and virtue he required of those who claimed political freedom gave his republicanism a strongly aristocratic bias.

The first assignment he undertook as government publicist was some observations on the situation in Ireland published in May 1649. Ever since the end of 1641 the Catholics of Ireland had been in revolt for their independence from the English parliament and freedom for their religion. Charles I had tried to use their rebellion for his own political purposes, and in 1649 the earl of Ormond, his lieutenant in Ireland, attempted to create an alliance against the commonwealth consisting of Royalists, Irish Catholics, and Scottish Presbyterians in Ulster. Milton's pamphlet was issued as an official statement, a government white paper, as it were. Along with the articles of Ormond's peace with the Irish rebels and other documents, it included Milton's commentary, which gave him an opportunity for a further statement of his political beliefs. In denouncing Ormond's policy of alienating Ireland from England's obedience, he echoed the common English prejudice that the Irish were a barbarous people "indocible and averse from all civility," who preferred their own "absurd and Savage Customes" to the benefits of a "civilizing Conquest."[33] Catholicism and the pope drew his anger as the subversion of all true religion and the embodiment of Antichrist. He boasted of how the English had destroyed the public superstitions of the Catholics, confining them "to the bare enjoyment of that which is not in our reach, their Consciences...."[34] Again he justified the army's purge of parliament in 1648 as a necessity to rid the Commons of its "rot'n Members" who sought to restore the king to

[32] See Don M. Wolfe, "Lilburne's Note on Milton," *Modern Language Notes*, vol. LVI, no. 5, which makes the questionable claim that Milton's failure to write against the Levellers indicates his friendship or sympathy for them. Wolfe points out that Lilburne's tract of 1652, *As You Were*, praises Milton and his advice to his countrymen in *A Defence of The English People*.

[33] *Observations upon The Articles of Peace, Made And Concluded with The Irish Rebels*, 1649, CPW, vol. III, pp. 304–305.

[34] Ibid., p. 309.

power. The king's execution he depicted as "an impartiall and noble piece of Justice" attesting that God was on its authors' side.[35] In answer to Ormond's disparagement of Cromwell, he extolled the general's high character and aristocratic credentials: "Cromwell...hath done in a few yeares more eminent and remarkable Deeds to found Nobility in his house, though it were lacking, then Ormond and all his Auncestors" could show from the record of their Irish exploits, "the widest scene of their glory."[36] The Presbyterian Scots in Ulster came in for repeated strictures for their seditious meddling in politics and readiness to oppress peaceful men's consciences. He defended the commonwealth's policy of toleration of Christians inoffensive in civil matters. It was after the early church first acquired worldly power, he pointed out, that its ruin began. Although the state wished to encourage sound doctrine and the power of godliness, the suppression of heresy, schism, and profaneness could not be the "work of the Civil sword, but of the spirituall which is the Word of God."[37]

Whom these observations on Irish affairs may have reached or influenced is unascertainable. The commitment they expressed to republicanism and to liberty of conscience in the qualified sense in which he understood this concept were enduring features of Milton's philosophy. He welcomed a kingless rule by heroic and virtuous men. His view of toleration implied that religious bodies were purely voluntary societies which must never be permitted to borrow the state's authority to coerce those of differing belief, and that the state must not molest them so long as they refrained from civil offense. These convictions associated him with the Independents who now held power. In Cromwell he could perceive the greatest representative of the new order. Even though at the time Cromwell was only one of the commonwealth's leaders, at most the first among equals, his heroic achievements as a military commander who had conquered every enemy proved that he enjoyed God's special favor. Before long Milton was to see the warrior Cromwell lead his army to Ireland where in the autumn of 1649 at Drogheda and Wexford he crushed the Irish Catholic rebels by a merciless slaughter which he called "a righteous judgment of God upon these barbarous wretches, who have imbrued their hands in so much innocent blood...."[38]

---

35 Ibid., pp. 311, 328.
36 Ibid., pp. 310–311, 317–320, 324.
37 Ibid., pp. 310–311, 317–320, 324.
38 *The Writings And Speeches of Oliver Cromwell*, 4 vols., ed. W. C. Abbott (Cambridge, Mass.: Harvard University Press, 1937–1947), vol. II, p. 127.

It was ironic that the new government Milton served was no less active than its predecessors in the regulation of the press. Alarmed by the circulation of false reports and attacks by its adversaries in newspapers, books, and pamphlets, it did its best to curb seditious printing. The Levellers complained vehemently of the Rump's and Council of State's censorship. "They may talk of freedom," said *The Second Part of Englands New-Chaines Discovered*, "but what freedom is there so long as they stop the Presse, which is indeed, and hath been so accounted in all free Nations, the most essential part thereof...."[39] In September 1649 parliament passed a stringent ordinance against scandalous books and pamphlets decreeing the licensing of all publications. Milton commented to his friend Hartlib that since the ordinance did not actually appoint licensers, anyone could bring out a book without license as long as it carried the author's or printer's name, as the law required. This might have enabled him to reconcile the ordinance with the precepts stated in *Areopagitica*.[40] On occasions he himself was assigned the task of licenser. If he felt uncomfortable in this position, he left no indication of it. For a year in 1651–52 he was responsible for licensing the semi-official weekly news sheet, *Mercurius Politicus*, though his performance of this role, we are told, was purely perfunctory.[41] In 1651 he licensed the *Racovian Catechism*, the exposition of faith of the Socinians, whose heresies included the denial of the Trinity. Parliament condemned the work as blasphemous and scandalous and ordered copies burned. Milton was examined about the circumstances of its appearance, and apparently explained that in approving its publication he was following his conviction that men should refrain from forbidding books.[42]

Another work he undertook at the Council of State's behest was a reply to *Eikon Basilike*, the supreme masterpiece of Royalist propaganda. The *Eikon*, subtitled *The Portraiture of His Sacred Majesty in His Solitude And Sufferings*, was a collection of essays, meditations, and prayers ascribed to Charles I. Although approved by the king

---

[39] This pamphlet is reprinted in Don M. Wolfe, *Milton in The Puritan Revolution* (New York: Thomas Nelson And Sons, 1941); the passage quoted is on p. 401.

[40] *Acts And Ordinances of The Interregnum*, ed. C. H. Firth and R. S. Rait, 3 vols. (London: HMSO, 1911), vol. II, pp. 245–254; Turnbull, p. 41; see the comments of Parker, vol. I, p. 354. David Masson, *The Life of John Milton Narrated in Connexion with The Political, Ecclesiastical, and Literary History of His Time*, 7 vols. (London: 1859–1894), vol. IV, pp. 116–118, though calling the press ordinance "severe enough," tries to palliate it by noting that the rigid application of the licensing system would have applied to newspapers and political tracts, not to books at large, and thus make it consistent with the principles in *Areopagitica*.

[41] Parker, vol. I, p. 394.

[42] Ibid., vol. I, p. 395; vol. II, p.994 n153.

and based on some of his papers, its real author, it later transpired, was John Gauden, an Anglican clergyman.[43] It contained Charles's review of various episodes since the beginning of the Long Parliament and presented him as a pious Christian, loving father, and conscientious ruler who cared for his people and bore his misfortunes with patience. The frontispiece showed him kneeling in prayer in his royal robes, a promised crown of eternal glory hovering above him. The book made its earliest appearance at the time of his execution and despite the government's efforts to suppress it, attained an enormous popularity. At least thirty-five editions were printed in England alone before the end of 1649 and there were foreign editions and translations as well. It tapped a deep vein of loyalty and veneration for kingship and made a vital contribution to the cult of the Christ-like royal martyr that came into being following the king's death.

In trying to discredit the *Eikon*, Milton took on an impossible task. He could scarcely hope that his indictment of Charles I would prevail against the sentiments of religious awe and pity for the deposed monarch which guaranteed the latter's book its extraordinary success. His reply, *Eikonoklastes (The Image Broken)* was published in October 1649, followed by a second edition in 1650, and consisted of a point-by-point refutation of the king's statements. The preface noted that the work had been assigned to him rather than chosen, and that he was not destitute of better and more certain means of acquiring fame than writing against a king. He knew that "the blockish vulgar" would admire anything ascribed to the king, even if it contained little but "the common grounds of tyranny and popery, drest up, the better to deceiv, in a new Protestant guise...." That it might be vain to write at all he likewise recognized, considering how much prejudice and envy it would stir up among "the common sort" to contradict the king's book. He had resolved nevertheless, he stated, to take up the gauntlet, even though a king's, in order to defend liberty and the commonwealth.[44]

Eikonoklastes made evident how low the English people had fallen in his estimation from the enlightened people whom he had celebrated in *Areopagitica*. The great popularity of the king's book increased his disillusion, which he revealed in numerous indications of contempt for the populace. The people, "exorbitant and excessive

---

[43] See Hughes's account of *Eikon Basilike*, CPW, vol. III, pp. 150–161, and the introduction by Philip A. Knachel to the Folger Library reprint, (Ithaca: Cornell University Press, 1966), which summarizes the salient details of the work's authorship and publication.

[44] *Eikonoklastes*, 2nd ed., 1650, CPW, vol. III, pp. 337, 338, 339.

in all their motions," were prone to idolize kings. Save for the few who still retained the old English love of freedom, they displayed "a besotted and degenerate baseness of spirit;" "imbastardized from the ancient nobleness of their ancestors," they were ready to fall flat and adore the image of a man who more than any previous British monarch strove to undermine the nation's liberties and make an art of tyranny. Even at the conclusion of the work he could not restrain a further outburst against the "irrationall, and Image-doting rabble," a "credulous...herd, begott'n to servility," who were ravished by the picture of the king at prayer as a sign of their own "voluntary and beloved baseness."[45] The age, too, was "graceless," while "ignorance and perverseness" had become "national and universal." He lamented that the wisdom, valor, constancy, and prudence which had united to rescue religion and liberty from tyranny were now reckoned as schism and faction.[46] His diatribe did not spare the Presbyterians either. An ungrateful, perverse generation, they who were the first to cry to God for deliverance from the king were now crying as loudly for the king against the men who had delivered them. They were so brazen as to acclaim the king's book, despite the fact that its withered arguments and reasons were the same ones their own party had earlier sought to confute.[47]

The bitterness of tone in *Eikonoklastes* was that of man who felt that his people had let him down and who, in spite of his affiliation with the victorious party, was all too conscious of being a member of a militant minority surrounded by hostility. Much of the work was devoted to countering the king's interpretation of events. Looking back on the civil war and its causes, Milton held that it lay in the power of parliament, as "the public reason" of a free nation, to decide what was law. Although relying occasionally for his defense of parliament on antiquarian precedents and the English past, more often and most characteristically he appealed to general principles of reason. Thus, in his denial of the king's authority to summon and dissolve parliaments at will, he cited "our ancient Law Books" which contained the "unwritt'n Law of common Right...ingrav'n in the hearts of our Auncestors....", as well as the royal coronation oath. On the other hand, he felt no doubt that a "better evidence" than the records of the law was "Reason;" and in contending that the king had no power to veto legislation by a negative voice, he inquired how it could stand with reason that the judgment of one man, and

45 Ibid., pp. 343–344, 601.
46 Ibid., p. 348.
47 Ibid., pp. 346, 347.

that not because he was a good or wise but simply as a king, "should outweigh the prudence, and all the vertue of an elected Parlament."[48]

At the most theoretical level Milton asserted his conviction of the ineluctable truth of the doctrine of popular sovereignty. Kings originated through the consent and suffrage of the people, who were to be governed as freemen by laws of their own making. They were entrusted servants, not masters, and as inheritors of their position, they in no way excelled others, being usually less wise and worthy than some of their subjects. It was never God's nor nature's intent, nor of any people not wholly barbarous, to exalt one person and his lineage for no merit but the mere chance of heredity "into an absolute and unaccountable dominion over them and thir posterity."[49] Milton pronounced the king's execution a supreme act of justice warranted by the laws of God and man. He would be happy, he said, if he could deliver the minds of Englishmen from longing to return to the captivity of kings from which the sword of justice had liberated them. He did not think the welfare and happiness of a nation depended on one man. National happiness consisted, rather, "in true Religion, Piety, Justice, Prudence, Temperance, Fortitude, and the contempt of Avarice and Ambition." Those who possessed these virtues needed no kings, but were "the architects of thir own happiness."[50]

This last sentiment reflected at its highest the moral outlook infusing Milton's politics. Yet he also stooped in *Eikonoklastes* to tactics that were less than creditable. In attacking the king as a tyrant, he ridiculed his expressions of piety as a pretense to cover his true designs. As further proof of this charge, he revealed that one of the prayers Charles I had used before his death came from "no serious Book," but from a "Heathen fiction." It was none other than Pamela's prayer from Sir Philip Sidney's *Arcadia*, a "vain amatorious Poem," which although full of worth and wit, was "among religious thoughts, and duties not worthy to be nam'd, nor to be read at any time without good caution; much less in time of trouble and affliction to be a Christians Prayer Book."[51] Sidney was a genuine Protestant hero who had fallen in the Elizabethan war with Spain; his *Apologie for Poetrie* contained as high and ethical a conception of the

---

48 Ibid., pp. 360, 402–403, 409–410.

49 Ibid., pp. 485–486.

50 Ibid., pp. 542, 584, 585, 586–592.

51 Ibid., pp. 361, 362–363. The grave charge that Milton himself was responsible for interpolating Pamela's prayer from *Arcadia* into the printing of later editions of *Eikon Basilike* has been largely disproved and is rejected by nearly all Milton scholars; see the discussion in Hughes' introduction, pp. 150–159, and Parker, vol. II, p. 969 n. 43.

poet's art as Milton's own; his romance, *Arcadia*, was a work pervaded by moral idealism. Milton knew all this. Moreover, the prayer the king took from *Arcadia* expressed a deep dependence on God for comfort in tribulation. If Milton had not identified it as Sidney's, no possible exception could have been taken to it. That he was willing to censure its use and to do so even at the price of maligning an eminent literary predecessor, compromised his own position and shows that he was none too scrupulous in his partisanship.

At its inception in 1649, the commonwealth faced a precarious future. Beside internal opposition, it had to reckon with the general hostility of foreign states, who condemned its execution of the king. In Scotland, moreover, the Scots proclaimed Charles II as the successor to his father on his acceptance of the National Covenant and prepared to reinstate him on the English throne by force as a Presbyterian monarch. Within the next three years, the situation had improved considerably. In the summer of 1650, following his conquests in Ireland, Cromwell led his army into Scotland to gain a great victory at Dunbar. Although much of Scotland was now subdued, a second Scottish army invaded England a year later in a last desperate effort in behalf of Charles II, only to be overthrown in September by Cromwell's veterans at the battle of Worcester. As a result of these developments the commonwealth's security was assured at home. At the same time, its military and naval prowess also won it the respect of other European states, so that it had little to fear from intervention abroad.

Despite the extreme revolutionary acts that gave it birth, the commonwealth was far from a radical regime. Those of its supporters in the sects and the army who looked to it for political, religious, and social reforms, for which there was much agitation in these years, found themselves profoundly disappointed by its conservatism. It stood for a policy of religious toleration within certain limits and the preservation of the republican order under parliament's rule, but turned a deaf ear to calls for reforms of the law and administration of justice, the abolition of compulsory tithes, and the reform of parliament and the electoral system. Apart from his opposition to tithes, Milton showed little interest in social or economic reforms, and while he had reservations about some of the government's actions, he was proud to be associated with the regicide republic. As a minor official of the Council of State, he was acquainted with a number of its chief men, some of whom he esteemed for their superior virtues in peace and war. A pair of sonnets he wrote in 1652 recorded his admiration for two of the commonwealth's principal figures. The first, to Cromwell, praised him as "our chief of men" and the instrument of God's work, one who, "guided by faith and matchless fortitude," had made his glorious way through a cloud of war and detraction to peace and truth. It concluded with the admonition that "much remains to conquer still; peace hath its victories no less renowned than war," and urged Cromwell to help preserve liberty of conscience from the dangers still threatening it. The other sonnet was addressed to Sir Henry Vane the younger, like Cromwell a Puritan and a leading republican politician and administrator. It hailed him both as a wise statesman "than whom a better senator ne'er held the helm of Rome" and as religion's "eldest son," who understood, as few others did, the difference between spiritual and civil power. Milton's main emphasis in extolling his heroes was on their protection of the religious conscience from oppression by the state, and this was one of the strongest concern's binding him to the commonwealth.[52]

Milton's literary services to the revolutionary government culminated in his *Pro Populo Anglicano Defensio* (*A Defence of The English People*), which he wrote at the request of the Council of State against the attack on the commonwealth by the famous French scholar, Salmasius (Claude de Saumaise). Published in November 1649, Salmasius' *Defensio Regia pro Carolo I* (*A Royal Defence of Charles I*) was undertaken at the behest of Charles II, to whom it was dedicated. His treatise was an indictment of the king's trial and execution, which argued from the Bible, history, and classical sources that kings as divinely appointed sovereigns were not accountable to their subjects. Milton's answer, first published in February 1651, also appeared in several later editions, including a revised version of 1658. Composed in Latin for an international audience, it contributed more than any of his previous works to make his name widely known.[53] The effort of preparing it was probably the final strain that cost him his eyesight.

[52] "To The Lord General Cromwell;" "To Sir Henry Vane The Younger;" CF, pp. 326–328. It is a point of some interest that Vane, although a faithful and outstanding servant of the republic, had withdrawn from parliament for about six weeks at the time of the army purge and refused to take part in the king's trial, to which he was apparently opposed; see Violet Rowe, *Sir Henry Vane The Younger* (London: Athlone Press, 1970), p. 139.

[53] *A Defence of The English People* was the first of Milton's works as an advocate of the commonwealth to bear his name on the title page. *The Tenure of Kings And Magistrates* and *Eikonoklastes* contained only his initials. An English translation of the 1658 edition of the *Defence* is printed in CPW, vol. IV, pt. I; the Latin text with a parallel English translation is in *The Works of John Milton*, ed. Frank A. Patterson, 20 vols. (New York: Columbia University Press, 1931–1940), vol. VII.

Although he took great pride in the *Defence*, boasting later that he had vanquished Salmasius and left him broken in spirit and reputation,[54] it compares unfavorably with other political writings of the period. Not only is it repetitious and badly organized, but its method, which consisted of tiresomely quoting, paraphrasing, and answering Salmasius' many charges page by page and almost line by line, was not conducive to coherent exposition or systematic argument. Milton conducted his controversy, moreover, with an utter lack of civility. Throughout his work he showered his adversary with a stream of insults, calling him a pimp, slave, eunuch, fool, liar, madman, hypocritical atheist, dunghill Frenchman, and other such names, and ridiculing him as a henpecked husband in bondage to a tyrannical wife. Even by the standard of the bad manners that often prevailed at the time in the debates of the learned, Milton's polemical style was excessive and in poor taste. While for all these reasons the *Defence* is of little account for political theory, it tells much about his republican values and the standpoint from which he sought to demonstrate the commonwealth's legitimacy.

In this work too he reiterated his conviction that the regicide ranked as a noble and heroic deed deserving of eternal glory. By the trial and execution of the king the English people shook off an ancient superstition and were led by God to recover their liberty. He did not overlook his own role as the man the state's leaders had chosen before all others to be the republic's champion. This was only fitting, he believed, since from his early years he had eagerly pursued studies which impelled him "to celebrate, if not to perform, the loftiest actions...."[55]

Salmasius had likened kings to fathers, both of whom enjoyed divine sanction and authority. Milton rejected the analogy, arguing that while nature gave people the fathers who begot them, it was the people who created kings. Hence kings existed for the people, not the people for kings. The origin of kings and royal power lay in the people when they first gathered together to appoint laws and rulers for their mutual protection against injury.[56] He found support for the principle of popular sovereignty and royal accountability in the Bible and classical authors like Cicero as well as in such well known sixteenth-century Huguenot monarchomach treatises as Philippe du Plessis-Mornay's *Vindiciae contra Tyrannos (Defense of Liberty against*

---

[54] *A Second Defence of The English People*, 1654, CPW, vol. IV, pt. I, p. 549.
[55] *A Defence of The People of England*, pp. 302, 303, 305.
[56] Ibid., pp. 327, 472.

Tyrants) and François Hotman's *Franco-Gallia*.[57] Among the Jews, the kings of the Old Testament were subject to the people, whose rights derived from God. God had created men free, and both Christ and the gospel put political freedom on a firm basis along with religious liberty. Although Paul in the epistle to the Roman had said that there is no power but of God, this was true of any type of state and legitimate rule over men. The choice of the form of government, however, always belongs to the people. Paul had also prohibited resistance, but his words applied only to lawful authority. Kings and magistrates who acted contrary to law were thus not the ordinance of God, but tyrants who could be justly resisted.[58] He quoted Cicero and other ancient writers as proof of the fact that the authority of all magistrates comes from the people, and noted how the Greeks and Romans had glorified tyrannicides and granted them divine honors.[59]

Most of the texts and examples Milton deployed were among the commonplaces of political debate in the preceding century between the upholders and opponents of the doctrine of the divine right of kings. While turning them to his own anti-monarchical purpose, he added nothing to the stock of ideas on the subject. Compelled to follow Salmasius also into a discussion of English history, he propounded the image of the ancient constitution as one of immemorial freedom and supremacy of law, a vision of the past dear to common lawyers and many of the crown's opponents in the civil war.[60] He insisted on the great antiquity and authority of parliament extending far back into Anglo-Saxon times, maintaining that even the Norman Conquest had not extinguished English liberty, since William the Conqueror had sworn to respect the rights and laws of his subjects. That parliament as the people's representative had always been superior to the king and the latter always obliged to consent to parliament's acts was equally plain to him. Further, he contended that the House of Commons antedated the existence of the Lords, to which it was superior; invested with the power of the

[57] See on these sixteenth-century writers, who made a vital contribution to the development of resistance theory and constitutional limitation on kingship, Julian H. Franklin, *Constitutionalism And Resistance* (New York: Pegasus, 1969); the introduction to François Hotman, *Francogallia*, ed. Ralph E. Giesey and J. H. M. Salmon (Cambridge: Cambridge University Press, 1972); Quentin Skinner, *The Foundations of Modern Political Thought*, 2 vols. (Cambridge: Cambridge University Press, 1978) vol. 2, pt. 3, chaps. 8–9.

[58] Ibid., pp. 344–345, 356–357, 373–376, 383–384, 385–386, 420, 481, 659.

[59] Ibid., pp. 388, 438–439, 446–447.

[60] See J. G. Pocock, *The Ancient Constitution And The Feudal Law*, 2nd ed. (Cambridge: Cambridge University Press, 1987), which discusses this conception of the ancient constitution and its roots in ideas of custom and the common law.

whole people and therefore supreme, it was fully entitled to judge the king for his crimes.[61] Milton's picture of the English constitution as preserving an unbroken continuity of liberty down through the ages was totally uncritical. Although drawing on familiar medieval sources like Magna Carta, Bracton, and the *Modus Tenendi Parliamentum*, he was deficient in historical sense. In treating his materials as an advocate, not a scholar, he produced a caricature of the king's and parliament's position in the polity in earlier times.

Despite the attention he was forced to give to historical considerations, arguments founded on the idealization and normativity of the past were not really congenial to his mind. He was never respectful of precedent, as his frequently expressed contempt of custom showed, and was apt to view the history of earlier centuries as largely filled with errors and superstition. Accordingly, the most fundamental justification he advanced for the king's execution and the overthrow of the monarchy lay in the law of nature, which was identical with the law of God. Replying to Salmasius's question by what law or right Charles I was put to death and the government changed, he contended that they were done "By that law of Nature and God which holds that whatever is for the safety of the state is right and just." The law of nature was the reason innate in all minds which regarded the welfare of every people joined in mutual association. Milton construed this formulation, taken from Salmasius' own book and common in European thought in one form or another since the time of Cicero, to mean that the law of nature preserved the rights of the people when they subjected themselves to a king and empowered him to act for their own safety against tyranny and injury. For nature, he pointed out, "has always looked, as she now does, not to the dominion of one man or a few, but to the safety of all...."[62] He did not trouble to analyze the law of nature as a concept or explain who was to judge in contested cases when it was violated and the people's safety at risk. Although Salmasius interpreted the law of nature as prohibiting resistance and regicide, Milton's sense took it as self-evident that it constituted a norm fully sufficient to warrant the unprecedented acts that brought the commonwealth into existence.

[61] Ibid., pp. 480–482, 485–486, 493–494.

[62] Ibid., pp. 317–318, 422–425; for Cicero's classic definition of the law of nature, see *De Re Publica*, bk. III, cap. 22, and *De Legibus*. bks. I, cap. 6, II, cap. 4. Milton's *Defence* frequently cited Cicero, including *De Legibus*; except for the *Somnium Scipionis*, preserved in Macrobius' commentary, and scattered quotations in ancient sources, he could not have known *De Re Publica* because its text was lost until 1820 and even then only partially recovered.

In the *Defence*, Milton's commitment to republicanism was stronger and more overt than in any of his preceding works on behalf of the commonwealth. Although it may be true, as J. H. Hanford commented many years ago, that the entire gist of his republicanism may be found in some of the entries of his earlier reading recorded in his *Commonplace Book*, we can find no sign of his republican allegiance until the experience of revolution led him to make it a part of his political creed.[63] His acquaintance and early biographer, John Aubrey, said that he wrote against monarchy

> out of a pure zeale to the liberty of mankind, which he thought would be greater under a fre state than under a monarchiall government. His being so conversant in Livy and the Roman authors, and the greatness he saw donne by the Roman commonwealth, and the virtue of their great commanders induc't him to.[64]

According to Hobbes' *Leviathan* also, one of the most frequent causes of rebellion and dislike of monarchy was the reading of "the Greek and Latine writers, in their books and discourses of Policy," which led those unprovided with the "Antidote of solid Reason" to prefer popular government and praise tyrannicide.[65] Milton may well seem to be one of those whom Hobbes had in mind; yet it was chiefly political contingencies rather than the influence of classical literature that made him into a republican. Only when the Independents in parliament and the army were impelled to break the constitutional impasse by trying the king and abolishing kingship did republicanism become a real political alternative for English minds. All of the *Defence*'s reasoning against royal tyranny and in favor of popular sovereignty implied a republican solution. Milton asserted that republican government was better suited then monarchy to human conditions. The only ground he could conceive for kingship was if kings were superior to those they ruled. When men were equals, however, and this was nearly always the case, "they should rule alike and in turn." It was altogether improper "for all to be the slaves of one who is their equal, often their inferior, and usually a fool." He denied Salmasius' claim that monarchy was nearer to nature because

---

[63] See J. H. Hanford, "The Youth of Milton," and "The Chronology of Milton's Private Studies," in *John Milton Poet And Humanist* (Cleveland: Western Reserve University Press, 1966), pp. 67, 109. These essays were first published respectively in 1925 and 1921.

[64] John Aubrey, *Brief Lives*, ed. Andrew Clark, 2 vols. (Oxford, 1898), vol. II, p. 69.

[65] Thomas Hobbes, *Leviathan*, 1651, ed. W. G. Pogson Smith (Oxford: Clarendon Press, 1943), pp. 166. 252.

most nations were governed by kings. What nature commands was made evident in the practice of the wisest peoples rather than the greatest number. Thus the Greeks, Romans, Italians, and many others had all preferred government by nobles or the people to that of kings. He endorsed the opinion of the Roman writer Sulpicius Severus that "the name of king has ever been hateful to nearly all free peoples."[66]

The most revealing parts of the *Defence* are the one's in which Milton tried to rationalize the status of the commonwealth as a regime imposed by force without a popular mandate. Here his enduring faith in the principle of aristocratic virtue came to his aid to enable him to dismiss criticism of the government as an unrepresentative minority rule. Only the few care for liberty or could enjoy it, he admitted, and these were the wise and brave. It was the uncorrupted part of the House of Commons that had cooperated in the purge of parliament and acted with the army to save the state. Such "deserve to rule the rest, as men rule women." These members stood by their trust in protecting the state, even though deserted by a great part of the people who desired peace and slavery.[67] He was willing to avow, nevertheless, that the people did all this;

> for why should I not say that the act of the better, the sound part of the Parliament, in which resides the real power of the people, was the act of the people? If a majority in Parliament prefer enslavement...is it not right for a minority to prevent it if they can and preserve their freedom?[68]

He also defended the nobility of the men who made the commonwealth: some were noble in the usual sense of birth and lineage, others, self-made, became truly noble through their own toil and rectitude. As for the people, whom Salmasius derided, they included not only the populace, but all citizens of every degree. Among them the best consisted of the middle rank, which produced the greatest number of prudent men most knowledgeable in affairs, the remainder being diverted either by excessive wealth and luxury or by want and poverty from an understanding of law and government.[69] In this sentiment Milton was probably echoing Aristotle's opinion in the *Politics* that men neither too rich nor too poor make the best citizens. Taken up afterwards by Florentine republican writers of the

---

[66] *A Defence of The English People*, pp. 344, 366–367, 431–432.
[67] Ibid., pp. 332–333, 336, 343, 518.
[68] Ibid., p. 457.
[69] Ibid., pp. 319, 471.

sixteenth century, this Aristotelian view that the *mediocri* were the only people capable of governing and being governed became an important element in the early modern revival of republican thought.[70]

Milton's reasoning endowed the noble and virtuous with the power of the people in order to compel the submission of the corrupt and misguided majority. In thus defending the commonwealth, he did not abandon the doctrine of popular sovereignty, but gave it an aristocratic meaning to adapt it to the political reality of the government's position. He was still able, however, to justify the abolition of the House of Lords on populist grounds. Because the peers were sent by no constituency and represented only themselves, they should have no right over the people. On the other hand noblemen, if elected to parliament, could vote on behalf of their communities as members of the supreme assembly of the people.[71]

Milton ended the *Defence* with a solemn caution to his countrymen and the nation's new rulers. God had liberated them from tyranny and superstition, the two worst evils of human life. After the famous deed of regicide, they should do nothing mean or low, but only what was great and noble. Having conquered their enemies in war, they must show in peace that they could surpass others in resisting greed, luxury, and the temptations of success. Only if their courage in the fight against slavery was equalled by their justice and moderation in preserving their freedom would they prove worthy of what they had won and demonstrate that they had acted not out of self-seeking but from love of justice, honor, and their country. Should they do otherwise, their enemies' accusations would be confirmed and God would abandon them.[72]

Although *A Defence of The English People* attracted considerable attention and brought Milton a reputation in the European republic of letters, it had no detectable influence on political thought. The only response of intellectual weight it evoked came in some courteously critical comments by the Royalist writer, Sir Robert Filmer. Filmer objected to Milton's account of popular sovereignty and the origins of kingship and pointed to contradictions in his conception of the people. Observing that Milton set aside majorities and allowed the sounder and better part to represent the people, he

[70] Aristotle, *Politics*, bk. IV, chap. 11; and see the discussion of the *mediocri* in J. G. Pocock, *The Machiavellian Moment* (Princeton: Princeton University Press, 1975), pp. 298, 300, 302, 388.
[71] Ibid., pp. 471, 509.
[72] Ibid., pp. 535–536.

put the question, "If the sounder, the better, and the uprighter part have the power of the people, how shall we know, or who shall judge who they be?"[73] Thomas Hobbes, too, the greatest political philosopher of the age, read the *Defence* and later commented both on it and Salmasius's book:

> They are very good Latin both, and hardly to be judged which is better; and both very ill reasoning, hardly to be judged which is worse; like two declamations, *pro* and *con*, made for exercise only in a rhetoric school by one and the same man.[74]

The *Defence* indicated a sharp contraction in Milton's political horizon. His vision of the people had faded and he no longer regarded them in the light of the glowing hopes that pervaded *Areopagitica* written eight years before. He was compelled to single out a minority maintained by military power as the true incarnation of popular sovereignty and the representative of a higher national will blessed by providence. While his commitment to the new revolutionary regime remained very strong, his concluding warning showed that he was far from certain whether it would live up to the standards he set for it. As ever, the moral factor was decisive in shaping his political attitude. He held freedom to be a supreme value, and his own immense personal pride rebelled against subjection to kings, who were no better, and usually worse, than other men. But freedom was above all the moral quality of self-command of which few were capable. He was therefore willing for this minority, an aristocracy of virtue comprising the noble both by birth and merit, to govern the unenlightened majority who could not govern themselves. This was not only the dominant motive of his republicanism, but his solution to the dilemma of the commonwealth, whose rulers invoked the fiction of popular sovereignty while realizing that they would have been swept from power if the wishes of the English people were freely consulted.

---

[73] Sir Robert Filmer, *Observations Concerning The Originall of Government upon Mr. Hobs Leviathan, Mr. Milton against Salmasius, H. Grotius De Jure Belli*, 1652, in *Patriarcha And Other Political Works*, ed. Peter Laslett (Oxford: Blackwell, 1949), p. 252.

[74] Thomas Hobbes, *Behemoth, or The Long Parliament*, ed. Ferdinand Tönnies (London, 1889), pp. 163–184. Hobbes probably wrote this work, which was first published in 1682, soon after the Restoration.

Chapter 4

MILTON IN REVOLUTION:
REPUBLICANISM AND THE END
OF THE REVOLUTIONARY EXPERIMENT

Milton finished *A Defence of The English People* in the certainty that his vindication of liberty and the commonwealth was a deed worthy of the noble actions that created the English republic. As he reflected on the few replies and comments it evoked, he succeeded in convincing himself that his work had brought him renown throughout Europe as liberty's champion. His exaggerated sense of his fame and achievement provided a needed consolation in the personal tragedies that presently befell him. The couple of years following the *Defence*'s publication must have been among the darkest of his life. In February 1652 his blindness became total, a fact he attributed to the extreme strain on his eyes caused by writing the *Defence*. In May his wife Mary died in childbed at the age of twenty-seven after giving birth to a third daughter, Deborah. Their son, the fifteen-month old John, followed her to the grave a month later. Milton remained a sightless widower charged with the care of his three young children.

We know nothing of his feelings at the loss of his wife and son. The undated *Sonnet XIX*, "Methought I saw my late espoused saint," which describes the appearance of his dead wife to him in a dream, is very poignant in its references to her and to his own blindness. Its subject, though, may not have been Mary Milton, but her successor, Katherine Woodcock, who in November 1656 became his second wife. Unfortunately, she too died within sixteen months of their marriage, also in the aftermath of childbirth, leaving behind an infant daughter who survived for only a few weeks.[1]

---

[1] *Sonnet XIX* is printed in CF, pp. 415–416. Although Parker holds that its subject is Mary Milton (vol. I, p. 475), its allusions fit Katherine Woodcock better; see CF's editorial note reviewing the evidence, p. 415.

We do have, however, considerable evidence of his reaction to his blindness. It is instructive to compare it with that of another great artist to a similar calamity, Beethoven's loss of hearing. Beethoven noticed the earliest symptoms of his deafness in 1798 when he was twenty-eight, and by 1801, when he first spoke of it, he mentioned the depth of his unhappiness because "my noblest faculty, my hearing, has greatly deteriorated." Under the burden of his affliction, feelings of wretchedness, shame, despair, resignation, and defiance of fate were among the fluctuating moods his letters recorded. "For two years," he reported to his doctor friend Wegeler, "I have avoided almost all social gatherings because it is impossible for me to say to people, 'I am deaf'." In the intensely pathetic Heiligenstadt Testament, written to his brothers in 1802 in contemplation of suicide or an early death, he voiced his grief at the loss of the auditory faculty he had once possessed in the highest perfection, as well as his terror lest his condition become known and his humiliation at hearing nothing when someone called a song or musical sound to his attention. Although he said that his art had thus far withheld him from suicide, he admitted hastening joyfully toward an early death that would end his suffering. The composer, nevertheless, surmounted this terrible crisis. Growing ever more profound in musical expression, he discovered in his enormous power of creation a continuing source of energy and renewal that transcended his adversity.[2]

Milton showed far less sign of spiritual travail over his blindness. Indications of suffering may appear in several of the eight psalms he translated into English in August 1653. In one the psalmist calls out to God for pity in his dejection and weakness; he is consumed by grief and his eye "is waxen old and dark...." Both here and in the preceding psalm he also feels himself watched by enemies. In the main, nevertheless, the theme of confidence in the Lord prevails, and the last of these versions is a victorious paean to Jehovah's greatness.[3] Milton seems to have known how to come to terms quickly with the loss of his sight. Obviously, the fact that, like Beethoven, he was still able to work with the help of assistants made his condition more tolerable. The self-mastery and conviction of vocation that accompanied him throughout his life enabled him to interpret the blow not only as God's will for him, but as a

---

[2] I have taken these quotations from J. W. N. Sullivan, *Beethoven* (London: Jonathan Cape, 1937), pp. 106–118; see the author's discussion in chap. II.

[3] Milton's translations of Psalms 1–8 are in CF, pp. 402–408; for the passages cited, see Psalms 5, ll. 22–23, 6, ll. 3–4, and all of Psalm 8.

further confirmation of his prophetic mission. Of course, he could not avoid wondering whether God intended his blindness as a punishment, as political adversaries charged. In 1654, in his *Second Defence of The English People*, in a passage that dealt with his loss of sight, he called God to witness that he had repeatedly examined his thoughts and every corner of his life, but found nothing either in his motives or actions whose wickedness could bring this supreme misfortune on him. Hence he stood unmoved, he declared, neither discerning nor enduring the anger of God. He also found reassurance in ascribing the final onset of his condition to the labor of writing his first *Defence*, a solemn duty he had undertaken at the bidding of a divine monitor to the great benefit of the state. Moreover, he could liken himself to the famous sages and heroes of the past who were afflicted by blindness: to the patriarch Isaac, to Tiresias, Timoleon, Appius Claudius, the great Venetian doge Enrico Dandolo, and the Hussite leader John Zizka. Proudly he averred that "not blindness, but the inability to endure blindness is a source of misery." Although deprived of sight of the visible world, he was confident that everything true and essential in it remained present to his intellectual vision. He trusted to God's mercy and protection to turn his weakness into strength, and that through the darkness of his infirmity he would be clothed in light.[4]

These admirable and moving sentiments expressed Milton's deepest feelings about his blindness. The undated sonnet on the subject, "When I Consider How My Light Is Spent," reflected an equal serenity in the poet's conviction that he served God best by patiently bearing God's "mild yoke."[5] The same spirit was also present in the letter he wrote in 1654 to an admiring acquaintance, the Athenian Leonard Philaras, which described his malady. He had resigned himself that it was incurable, he said, yet by the kindness of providence his days were brightened by leisure, study, and the visits of friends, and he found comfort in believing that he saw not by his eyes "but by the guidance and wisdom of God," who had led him throughout his life.[6]

---

[4] *A Second Defence of The English People*, 1654, CPW, vol. IV, pt. I, pp. 584–590. The original Latin text of this work is printed with a parallel English translation in *The Works of John Milton*, ed. Frank A. Patterson, 20 vols. (New York: Columbia University Press, 1931–1940), vol. VIII.

[5] *Sonnet XVI*, CF, p. 330; scholars have attributed the poem either to the year 1652 or 1655.

[6] Printed in CPW, vol. IV, pt. II, pp. 868–870.

Despite his handicap, Milton continued in his official employment, although with lightened duties. In April 1653, another shock struck the political scene when Cromwell and the army forcibly expelled the Rump, thus putting a temporary end to what remained of the Long Parliament. Not only was the Rump highly unpopular in the country, but it had increasingly lost favor with its own supporters because of the reputed corruption of some of its members and its failure to enact reforms. It had been expected to produce a reformed electoral law and then dissolve itself to make way for a new representative. Instead, it clung to power, seemingly bent on its own perpetuation. Despite the pressure from the army's officers to complete its work, it proceeded dilatorily with a scheme that would apparently have allowed a number of its members to retain their seats while filling up vacancies through new elections in reapportioned constituencies. The impatient officers were determined, however, that the Rump must go. Finally, enraged by its conduct, Cromwell, himself a member, denounced the body in a scalding speech and calling in a troop of soldiers, he ordered the parliament dissolved.

This totally unconstitutional act, more drastic even than the earlier purge, eliminated from public life a number of the republican statesmen Milton most respected, who refused to countenance the army's action. Furthermore, it left a political vacuum, which Cromwell and his council of officers first tried to fill by calling a parliament of members nominated by themselves. When this expedient failed owing to the parliament's divisions, they instituted a new polity, the protectorate, based on a written constitution, the Instrument of Government. Under its provisions, Cromwell held the quasi-regal office of lord protector for life, ruling England with the help of a council of state and an elected parliament. Established at the end of 1653, the protectorate evolved steadily toward kingship. In 1657 its second parliament urged Cromwell to become king, but he refused, wary of the army's reaction to such a step. Had he lived much longer, he might well have assumed the throne as a constitutionally limited hereditary monarch. He was given the power to name his successor as protector, however, and a second chamber with a Cromwellian peerage equivalent to the former House of Lords was also introduced. This regime lasted not quite six years, surviving Cromwell's death in September 1658 by only eight months. It was supported by a variety of conservative and moderate men who were willing to cooperate in the hope of restoring political stability, and by many pious Independents and separatists to whom Cromwell appeared a leader appointed by providence to preserve the cause of the godly. Ultimately, of course, it rested on the power of the army.

91

It met with strong opposition from the politicians of the Rump and the republicans, who were outraged at Cromwell's use of military force and condemned him for usurping personal power. Some Baptists and other sectarians of the millenarian Fifth Monarchist movement, convinced that Christ would shortly return in power to rule the world with his saints, likewise opposed it because Cromwell had torn the crown from Christ's head to put it on his own.[7]

Throughout these changes and whatever his misgivings, Milton remained Secretary for Foreign Tongues, serving the protectorate's Council of State as he had previously done the commonwealth's. In May 1654 he published *Pro Populo Anglicano Defensio Secunda* (*A Second Defence of The English People*), a sequel to the earlier *Defence*, replying to an attack on both himself and the government in a Royalist polemic, *Regii Sanguinis Clamor ad Coelum adversus Parricidas Anglicanos* (*The Cry of The Royal Blood to Heaven against The English Parricides*). The latter, an able piece of propaganda which continued Salmasius' denunciation of the king's execution and its perpetrators, appeared anonymously in 1652 from a Dutch press in The Hague. On quite slender evidence Milton attributed it to Alexander More, a French Protestant minister and associate of Salmasius who had held academic posts in Geneva and the Dutch republic. Even though friends advised him that More did not write *The Cry of the Royal Blood*, he persisted in this identification and reviled More throughout the *Second Defence* as its author. A few years after the Restoration, it became known that the true author was Peter Du Moulin, an English Royalist clergyman; all that More contributed was the dedicatory letter to Charles II. This was another of the occasions on which Milton showed himself deficient in scruple when engaged in combat with a political opponent.[8]

The *Second Defence* was an extraordinary production in several respects. Liberty was its overarching theme, and never did Milton rise to greater heights of eloquence than when standing forth in this work as its champion. At the same time its arguments were encumbered and its tone impaired by its unremitting abuse of Alexander More, particularly in its repeated references to his sexual misdemeanors, on which Milton dwelt with relish. True, he had an excuse for indulging in these insults, since *The Cry of The Royal Blood*

[7] Blair Worden, *The Rump Parliament* (Cambridge: Cambridge University Press, 1974), chaps. 13–17, and Austin Woolrych, *Commonwealth to Protectorate* (Oxford: Clarendon Press, 1982), contain a detailed account of these developments.

[8] For Milton's failings in dealing with the question of More's alleged authorship of *The Cry of The Royal Blood*, see Don M. Wolfe's introduction to CPW, vol. IV, pt. I, pp. 274–282.

had vilified him and impugned his character. It had pictured him as entirely unworthy to stand against Salmasius, as a sightless monster and worm out of the dungheap, a man expelled from Cambridge because of his disgraceful conduct, and a violator of all laws who went from the disruption of marriage to the dissolution of kingdoms. Its whole last chapter was an assault on the "foul rascal and parricide," Milton, whom it bedecked with many coarse epithets and called a criminal and public enemy deserving of the gallows.[9] With such a justification to respond in kind, Milton gave back better than he received; but his tasteless concentration on More's sexual foibles detracted from the effectiveness of his reply.

The need to vindicate his character from misrepresentation was the reason for the most remarkable feature of the *Second Defence*, the amount of information Milton gave about himself. In none of his previous writings did he speak of himself so fully. Beside presenting what amounted to a concise autobiography, he sprinkled self-references throughout the work. In his exordium he claimed to outstrip the orators of every age in the grandeur of his theme and to be addressing all the most influential men, cities, and nations everywhere. Having borne off the spoils of honor in his former combat with Salmasius, he was disseminating liberty to all the world on behalf of the entire human race. In this way he made himself into the focal point of his work.[10] Further on, as I have previously noted, he repelled the accusation that his blindness was a punishment from God. Here he stressed that he was never influenced by ambition but acted solely from motives of duty, honor, and devotion to his country.[11] When he came to describe his life, he explained that he did so to persuade both learned men in neighboring countries and his own people that he was incapable of dishonorable conduct and had always lived far removed from vice or crime. I have already cited parts of the ensuing narrative in earlier chapters. The information supplied went well beyond the polemical needs of the occasion. He reviewed his honorable family background, his precocious childhood and education at Cambridge, where he was held in high regard. After mentioning his private studies, he described his continental travels and the marks of esteem he had received from many distinguished men. Finally, he surveyed his previous writings dedicated to the cause of liberty. Of the three kinds of liberty, ecclesiastical, domestic,

---

[9] An abridged English translation of *The Cry of The Royal Blood* is in CPW, vol. IV, pt. II; for the passages cited, see pp. 1045, 1050, 1051, 1078–1081.

[10] *A Second Defence*, pp. 554, 555, 557–558.

[11] Ibid., p. 587.

and civil, which were necessary to civilized life, his earlier writings dealt with the first two, his later ones with the third. His aim was to show that "true and substantial liberty" was an inward possession, achieved not by the sword "but by a life rightly undertaken and rightly conducted." In the services he had rendered to the church and state he disclaimed any desire for personal advantage. While others sought for gain or office, he looked only for a good conscience and the respect of good men.[12]

In More's reply to the *Second Defence* denying his authorship of *The Cry of The Royal Blood*, he ridiculed Milton for singing his own praises. Referring to his bragging, pride, and haughtiness, he observed that Milton wished to be thought the most exalted of men.[13] More was not far wrong in this criticism. Although the highmindedness of Milton's motives cannot be doubted, it is also evident that his self-portrayal reflected the great unconscious egotism, amounting almost to self-worship, which was an inherent part of his character.

The political core of the *Second Defence* was a reaffirmation of the people's right to overthrow tyrants and an exhortation to the Cromwellian regime to live up to the highest moral ideals. Equally apparent was the casuistry Milton found it necessary to use in order to square his arguments with the principle of popular sovereignty. He was forced to redefine and narrow the notion of the "people" to make it accord with the existing political situation. The theory of liberty and government he thereby propounded was all the more aristocratic in character as its populist trappings fell away. In reiterating his uncompromising conviction that parliament was fully competent to punish the king as a tyrant, he insisted that it did not need to consult the people or multitude in a matter exceeding their understanding. Indeed, as possessor of supreme power, parliament itself was the people. Although admitting that the Independents were a minority, he claimed for them a superiority of merit which entitled them to power. According to his judgment, nothing was more natural, just, or beneficial to the human race than that

> the lesser obey the greater, not the lesser number the greater number, but the lesser virtue the greater virtue, the lesser wisdom the greater wisdom. Those whose power lies in wisdom, experience, industry,

---

12 Ibid., pp. 611–627.

13 An English translation of parts of More's reply, *Alexandri Mori...Fides Publica, contra Calumnias Ioannis Miltoni* (*The Public Faith of Alexander More...against The Calumnies of John Milton*), 1654, is printed in CPW, vol. IV, pt. II; see p. 1109 for the passages cited.

and virtue will...however small their number, be a majority and prove more powerful in their suffrages everywhere than any mere number, however great.[14]

Thus, while perhaps not abandoning the conception of rights as the foundation of the political order, he subordinated it to the principle of virtue as the prime requisite of true citizenship and participation in the polity. And it should be noted that for him this virtue was by no means identical with religious grace or regeneration; it was very largely a product of natural moral qualities proper to humankind whether pagan or Christian.

In keeping with this view he lavished eulogies on a number of individual leaders of the republic for their outstanding virtue. The first he named was John Bradshaw, the president of the court that had tried the king: a man sprung from a noble line, of lofty spirit and pure morals, intent solely on the public good, steadfast of mind and worthy of trust in every kind of fortune, generous to recognize any sort of genius, whose noble deeds in behalf of the state had won him eternal glory. He went on to speak of Fairfax, the army commander, gifted by nature and divine favor with supreme courage, supreme modesty, and supreme holiness, and then more briefly of various other men, both army officers and politicians, whom he singled out for their exceptional merits.[15] It was ironic that some of those extolled in this gallery of notables, including Bradshaw and Fairfax, were no longer active in government because of their opposition to Cromwell's one-person rule. Equally ironic was the omission from this list of Sir Henry Vane the younger, whose virtue Milton had celebrated in a sonnet only two years before; the republican Vane had also broken with Cromwell over the expulsion of the Rump and establishment of the protectorate.

Of all the statesmen of the republic Milton reserved his most extravagant praises for Cromwell, whom he called the liberator of his country and a man of supreme excellence. He stressed, of course, as he always liked to do about a man when possible, the "renowned and illustrious stock" from which Cromwell came. The virtues he ascribed to him were a composite of the true Miltonic hero: devotion to religion and an upright life, steadfastness in counsel, magnificent leadership in war. Before he commanded others he had learned to be a commander and victor over himself, subduing all the enemies in his own breast – vain hopes, fears, desires. His military camp was a school of religion and piety, his soldiers, unlike those of typical

---

[14] *A Second Defence*, pp. 634, 635, 636; I have slightly altered the translation.
[15] Ibid., pp. 637–639, 669, 675–678.

armies, disciplined in the performance of their duty. No preeminent general among the ancients, neither Cyrus nor Epaminondas, exceeded him as a leader of men. As long as he lived England was safe, because God fought on his side. Milton defended Cromwell's forcible dissolution of parliament and attributed his ascendancy in the state to his unsurpassed virtue. Nothing was more agreeable to reason or pleasing to God, he maintained, than that the fittest man should rule. This was the case of Cromwell, the nation's greatest citizen and author of its liberty who, spurning the name of king, had assumed the government as the father of his country.[16]

Along with his panegyric of the Lord Protector, Milton tendered him some frank and liberal advice. In effect, his words conveyed a solemn warning against succumbing to the temptations of supreme power, which, he said, would test Cromwell to the utmost. To the latter had been entrusted the liberty of his country. If he failed to cherish it and violated others' liberty, he would lose his own and become a slave. He must therefore rule with wisdom and modera- tion, leading the people from base customs to a higher standard of morality and discipline, resisting the allurements of wealth and pleasure. He should also take into his counsels as collaborators the men who had been his comrades in helping to free the state from tyranny. This was probably a plea for Cromwell to conciliate and share power with the republicans who had been alienated by his expulsion of the Rump and assumption of a quasi-regal authority. On the subject of religion, Milton recommended the total separation of church and state and the removal of all power from the former, including the abolition of compulsory tithes. He also urged Cromwell to make better and fewer laws and to take measures for the education and moral development of the young. To these prescrip- tions he added that in order for the truth to flourish, those engaged in free inquiry should be permitted to publish their thoughts without any interference. Finally, with regard to toleration, he bade Cromwell not to side with any faction that would oppress the consciences of others, since all citizens in the state had an equal right to freedom.[17]

Milton's work ended with an impassioned exhortation to his countrymen concerning liberty. In this peroration, addressed chiefly to the supporters of parliament, the commonwealth, and the protectorate, he preached much the same message as in his earlier *Defence of The English People*. Liberty, he told them, depended on

---

[16] Ibid., pp. 666–669, 671–672.
[17] Ibid., pp. 673–675, 678–680.

character rooted in true virtue. Unless piety, justice, and temperance were lodged deep in their souls, they would surely lose the liberty they had won in war. "Many men," he said, "has war made great whom peace makes small." If they neglected the arts of peace, leaving war as their sole virtue, their liberty would turn into servitude. Only by expelling ignorance and superstition from religion and avarice and ambition from their lives could they destroy the tyranny within themselves. To conquer this tyranny was the warfare of peace, whose victories were more glorious than those of war. Should they fail in this effort, their earlier conquests in the field would be in vain, for they would have defeated the Royalists only to become like them in their vices.[18]

Without mincing words, he went on to admonish them that freedom of elections to parliament was futile if they chose bad men who used office corruptly for self-enrichment. Such thieving servants were unfit to be guardians of liberty or caretakers of the state. These comments were meant as a swipe at the corruption that had marred the reputation of the Long Parliament. Those unworthy of liberty, he stated, should not possess it. By the decree of nature itself, freedom was only for the pious, just, and temperate. Those lacking these virtues were slaves to their own lusts; unable to rule themselves, they should ruled by others. As for himself, he said proudly, he had borne witness in defending liberty at home and abroad, erecting a lasting monument to the glory of his countrymen. If in spite of his efforts the nation failed to be worthy of itself, posterity would condemn it, even though there was not lacking one (meaning himself) who could rightly counsel, encourage, and inspire, and bestow immortal praise on noble deeds and those who performed them.[19]

Milton's conclusion attained a loftiness of thought which exalted himself and his writing in the same breath with liberty. Soaring far above mundane political realities, it constituted eloquent testimony to the idealistic standard that remained his constant measure in judging politics. While most republicans indicted the protectorate as an illegitimate regime, his own republican values did not hinder him from being Cromwell's most ardent advocate because in the latter he discerned supreme fitness to govern. In his tribute to liberty he formulated his conception of it more fully than in anything else he wrote. This conception was profoundly moral, as it had always been. Nevertheless, his attitude had narrowed considerably compared with

[18] Ibid., pp. 680–683.
[19] Ibid., pp. 683–686.

his earlier views, when his enthusiasm for the revolutionary cause was at its peak. The people having fallen so far below his expectations for them, he was now largely indifferent to the common political rights of citizens to appoint their governors and to the freedom of parliamentary elections as one of these rights. No less indifferent to him was the securing of parliament's authority and independence. He could not overlook the fact that if his countrymen were free to choose, they were likely to bring back monarchy and reject the religious tolerance he held so dear. Accordingly, his attention focused more than ever on the virtuous few. Liberty as he understood it was a personal attribute independent of circumstances. Of course, he was well aware that in one of its meanings it signified freedom from external constraint. But this freedom he would allow only to good men. The essence of liberty thus consisted of obedience to one's higher self, the self that had subdued its passions to right reason and ordered its desires and aims in accord with piety, justice, temperance, and fortitude. It is true that he remained passionately committed to freedom of conscience (though only for Protestants) and strongly opposed to the censorship of books. Yet it was the inward impediments to liberty, not the trammels imposed on its exercise from without, that most preoccupied him. In this sense, it lay beyond politics and was a possession of the soul. Liberty was therefore identical with virtue. The virtuous alone were truly free and it was only for them that rights existed. The carnal majority enslaved to their baser selves were unfit for liberty and would misuse it. Whatever their number, it was only right, as God and nature ordained, that they should be ruled by the virtuous. This was the ultimate lesson on liberty Milton wished to teach the people in celebrating the deeds that had delivered them from royal tyranny.

There was a sequel to the *Second Defence*. In October 1654 Alexander More published a refutation, supplying proofs that he had not written *The Cry of The Royal Blood* and charging Milton with lies and slander.[20] To this Milton replied in *Pro Se Defensio* (*Defence of Himself*), a tedious tract devoid of political interest.[21] In this rebuttal he performed the sophistical feat of refusing to admit his error by arguing that through his association with *The Cry*, More in any case

---

[20] *The Public Faith of Alexander More…against The Calumnies of John Milton*, 1654; in the following year More published a further answer to Milton, *Supplementum Fidei Publicae* (*Supplement to The Public Faith*), extracts from which are printed in CPW, vol. IV, pt. II, to which Milton replied in an addendum at the conclusion of *Defence of Himself*; see the following note.

[21] *Defence of Himself*, 1655, CPW, vol. IV, pt. II. The Latin text with parallel English version is printed in *The Works of John Milton*, vol. IX.

bore the entire responsibility for the work. Only once or twice in passing did he incidentally concede that More was not in fact the author, but this acknowledgement was lost amidst the accusations and vilification he continued to heap on his adversary.[22] Throughout his answer he never let it be forgotten that he wrote not for personal reasons but for the honor of his country. Denying that he had praised himself, he only praised himself the more by claiming to be singularly favored by God who had called him "above all others to the defence of liberty," a cause he had bravely vindicated. As in the *Second Defence*, confident that he had discharged a duty salutary to both church and state, he recognized no distinction between "the cause of my country and myself," since they were one and the same.[23]

Although he cut down considerably on his work for the Council of State in the later 1650s, Milton's intellectual labors in no way diminished. Despite his blindness, his energies and ambition to create remained as powerful as ever. He was then living in a house in Westminster to which he had moved from his official lodgings several years before, and had the help of readers and amanuenses, so that he was able to continue his studies and writing. Among the projects he undertook at this period was the compilation of a Greek and Latin dictionary. To it probably belongs also the beginning of *Paradise Lost*. Still another considerable task to which he devoted himself was an exposition of Christian doctrine which he considered one of his major works. This Latin theological treatise, largely completed by 1660, stands as lasting evidence that he was as much a rebel in religion as in politics.

He wrote *De Doctrina Christiana* (*Christian Doctrine*) in order to present a full statement of his religious beliefs. Had the Restoration not supervened, he would doubtless have published it in his lifetime. In the reaction that followed, however, he would have incurred great danger in letting his opinions appear in print. Hence the work remained undiscovered till long after his death and was not published till 1825.[24] By then he was a revered poet and the order for publication came from George IV. The treatise was a lengthy one, divided into two books, the first on faith and the knowledge of God,

[22] See ibid., pp. 712–713, 754, for his admission that More was not the author of *The Cry*.

[23] Ibid., pp. 735, 794, 796.

[24] *De Doctrina Christiana* is printed in English translation in CPW, vol. VI, with an introduction by the editor, Maurice Kelley, who discusses its date and composition, pp. 3–40; the Latin text with parallel English translation is printed in *The Works of John Milton*, vols. XIV–XVII.

the second on charity or practice and the worship of God. The prefatory epistle, addressed to all churches and Christians everywhere in a feeling of "universal brotherhood," outlined his personal approach to the problem of religious knowledge. Like the generality of Protestants, he looked to the Bible as the sole authority of religious truth, for only there did God reveal himself. Pursuant to this fundamental Protestant principle, he crammed his pages "even to overflowing," as he said, with scriptural quotations to buttress his religious conceptions. His biblical study led him, however, to conclusions of the most extreme individualism from which nearly all Protestants would have shrunk with horror. Since God's revelation of the way of salvation was directed to each individual believer, he held that everyone must work out his faith for himself; no one could or should depend on the belief of another. This claim enforced the necessity that every person must be free to examine any doctrine and openly discuss and publish his opinion. Without such freedom, Milton held, "there is no religion and no gospel," and violence alone would prevail.[25] Echoing his former argument in *Areopagitica*, he reassured the friends of truth that free inquiry and discussion would bring no harm to the church; on the contrary, they were absolutely essential to increase the light of truth. He had no fear of heresy. What he feared and opposed, rather, was the blind acceptance of human opinions and church traditions reflecting the perversion of truth over the centuries since the time of the apostles. Consonant with this attitude he voiced his contempt for the "irrational bigots" who branded with the hateful name of heresy whatever did not agree with conventional belief. Yet nothing except what contradicted Holy Scripture, he pointed out, could correctly be called heresy, and it was Scripture alone that he followed. The blunders and distortions committed by orthodox writers, moreover, had taught him to agree with their opponents whenever the latter agreed with the Bible.[26]

Milton's radical individualism thus made the mind and conscience of each believer the sole and ultimate judge of religious truth. He explained this position further in a chapter on the Bible. While recognizing that there were right methods for interpreting Scripture which entailed knowledge and learning, he likewise held that its meaning would be absolutely clear even to uneducated believers who studied it diligently. But in any case, every believer was entitled to interpret Scripture for himself, and no visible church or magistrate had the right to impose an interpretation on the consciences of

---

[25] *Christian Doctrine*, pp. 117, 118, 121.
[26] Ibid., pp. 117, 118, 121, 122, 123, 124.

others. Furthermore, Scripture was double, external and internal. The first consisted of the written word, the second of the holy spirit which God gave believers. It was the latter, "the individual possession" of each person, that had to be "the preeminent and supreme authority." If believers disagreed about the sense of Scripture, then they were obliged to tolerate each other until God revealed the truth to all.[27]

Although according primacy to the holy spirit, Milton's approach to Scripture also left a large role for reason in understanding biblical truth. His religion was so unorthodox in its blend of beliefs that it set him apart from all existing churches. He remained a church of one in which he was his own minister. Beside rejecting dogmas the Christian church had professed for centuries, he also dissented from the Calvinist theology which had dominated English Protestantism from the later sixteenth century up until his own time. His treatise propounded a number of major heresies or divagations from generally accepted Protestant teaching which he defended on both scriptural and rational grounds. These were antitrinitarianism, materialism, Arminianism, and mortalism. The first denied the orthodox doctrine of the Trinity affirming the co-equality and co-eternity of the Father, Son, and Holy Spirit. Instead of three persons in one, he placed the Son and Holy Spirit in subordination to the Father, the supreme, eternal, self-existent God who is one "in the numerical sense in which human reason always understands it."[28] The second held that God did not create the world out of nothing, but out of matter taken from himself. One of the implications of this opinion was that matter was intrinsically pure and holy rather than a source of evil. The third maintained, contrary to the Augustinian-Calvinist doctrine of predestination, that God had left humanity with free will to obtain salvation and did not by his eternal decree predestine anyone to damnation. The fourth affirmed the unity and interdependence of body and soul, with the conclusion that the soul was therefore mortal and died with the body to remain in its lifeless state until the resurrection and last judgment.[29]

Any one of these doctrines would have stamped Milton as a dangerous heretic in the eyes of nearly all contemporary Protestant denominations. Together they prove that he was a spiritual rebel

[27] Ibid., pp. 578, 582, 583, 584, 587.

[28] Ibid., p. 216.

[29] Kelley's introduction, pp. 43–99, surveys Milton's principal doctrines and heresies and includes references to the interpretations of other scholars, who have not been in agreement on some aspects of Milton's divagations from orthodoxy; see also the discussion in Harry F. Robins, *If This Be Heresy. A Study of Milton And Origen* (Urbana: University of Illinois Press, 1963), chap. 3.

unafraid to depart in fundamental ways from the prevailing creed of the churches. Despite the presence during the English revolution of numerous authors – Socinians, spiritualists, pantheists, mortalists, and Arminians – who expressed particular beliefs similar to his own, few embraced such a broad spectrum of unorthodox opinions. Another example of the latter, though it was not a heresy, was his elaborate defense of polygamy. In a chapter on marriage which reiterated the position expressed in his divorce tracts, he also devoted considerable space to proving that polygamy was sanctioned by Scripture and in no way a sin.[30]

How Milton came by his heretical beliefs is impossible to determine. Convinced of their truth by his long examination of the Bible, he must also have been influenced by his reading of the heterodox literature of early Christianity and the Reformation era. Close resemblances exist, for example, between his theological doctrines and those of the unorthodox church father Origen.[31] In the course of his studies he would also have come to know some of the antitrinitarian writings produced by the Socinians of the sixteenth and seventeenth centuries. Although proof is lacking that he was directly acquainted with the work of Servetus, who was executed in 1552 at Calvin's instigation for his antitrinitarianism, a number of parallels between his and Milton's views have been discerned.[32] On the subject of free will, he was familiar with the controversial literature in the Dutch republic, in which the liberal theology of the rationalistic Arminians challenged the Calvinist dogma of predestination maintained by the Dutch Reformed church. In regard to mortalism or soul-sleeping, he could have known both English and continental writings that maintained this heretical tenet. From these and kindred sources he might have found part of the inspiration that led him toward his unorthodox conclusions.[33]

Christian Doctrine contained a chapter on the gospel and Christian liberty which did not apply the latter principle to the political realm. Its principal thesis was that the gospel and new covenant of Christ

---

[30] *Christian Doctrine*, pp. 356–358; see Leo Miller, *Milton among The Polygamophiles* (New York: Loewenthal Press, 1974), for an account of the intellectual background of Milton's defense of polygamy.

[31] See Robins, chap. 4.

[32] Martin Larson, "Milton And Servetus. A Study in The Sources of Milton's Theology," *Publications of the Modern Language Association*, vol. XLI, no. 4 (1926).

[33] See Kelley's discussion of Milton's sources and probable indebtedness to heterodox writers in *Christian Doctrine*, pp. 107–109, and the treatment of his mortalism in Norman T. Burns, *Christian Mortalism from Tyndale to Milton* (Cambridge, Mass.: Harvard University Press, 1972, chap. 4.

had abolished the entire Mosaic law and enfranchised believers with spiritual liberty which required freedom of conscience in all religious matters. In arguing for freedom of conscience he also deviated from the mainstream Protestantism of his day, which was certainly not disposed to toleration. A subsequent chapter on particular churches defined the church as a voluntary society and maintained that religious bodies ought to be unmolested and exempt from all external authority in their worship and belief. It also condemned tithes and other forced payments to ministers of religion, contending that the latter should support themselves either from freely offered contributions or by work in a trade or profession.[34] Another chapter on church discipline held that not only ministers but all believers should be free to preach, exhort, and prophesy according to their talent; women, though, were to keep silent in church. Insisting on the complete separation of church from state, Milton declared that the civil power could have no place in enforcing ecclesiastical discipline; churches could use only spiritual weapons and those only against their own members. Discussing the duties of magistrates, he asserted that while they ought to protect religion, they ought not to enforce it and were forbidden to subject religious people to any sort of compulsion.[35] As for the people's duties to magistrates, they owed the latter obedience, but not when they became tyrannical or issued wicked commands.

Milton called his treatise on Christian doctrine his "dearest and best possession."[36] Its teachings demonstrated the exceptional independence of his religious thought and the greatness of his desire to promote the removal of all coercion in religion. On this one subject, he was more consistent over the years than he ever was in his political opinions.

Cromwell's death in September 1658 doomed the protectorate to an early end. His son and successor as protector, Richard Cromwell, was neither a soldier, a leader, nor experienced in any office, and he lacked the capacity to control the forces his father had known how to dominate. This was a regime, in any case, that governed without consent and in dependence on the army. In January 1659 Richard convened a parliament to which a number of republicans were elected who did their best to challenge the protectorate's legitimacy. Frictions also arose between Richard's ministers and supporters who

[34] Ibid., pp. 525–526, 536, 538, 541, 597–599, 601–602.
[35] Ibid., pp. 608–609, 612–613, 797–798, 800–801.
[36] Ibid., p. 126.

wished to reestablish civil authority over the army, and the army's principal officers determined to remain a power unto themselves. These rifts destroyed the protectorate. In April the army forced the dissolution of parliament and pressured Richard to retire to private life. Not presuming to assume the government themselves, they heeded the urging of the republicans and recalled the Rump, the old vestige of the Long Parliament which they had expelled six years before. In May nearly fifty of its members resumed their seats at Westminster in response to the army's summons.

These events and growing divisions were signs that the English revolution was entering its death throes. Milton, however, had no suspicion of the fact. He remained an official of Richard Cromwell's Council of State, still occasionally drafting diplomatic correspondence, and continued his service under the newly restored Rump, whose recall he greeted with enthusiasm. What primarily occupied his mind during these months of increasing instability was the question of liberty of conscience, a matter second to none among his most cherished concerns. Despite his warm support of Oliver Cromwell, he had never been happy with the latter's religious policy. As Lord Protector Cromwell had certainly done much to implement religious toleration in a society most of whose members, including many Puritans, were far less tolerant than himself. He had permitted a broad latitude for the peaceable coexistence of Presbyterians, Independents, Baptists, and other religious groups, provided they did not adhere to popery or prelacy or make their beliefs a pretext for licentious practices. At the same time, though, he refused to abdicate the state's responsibility for assuring the fitness of parochial ministers and of providing for their maintenance. Concerning tithes, which Milton abhorred, he was adamant in resisting the agitation of sectarians who cried out for their abolition as an imposition on the consciences of the godly. In 1656, in response to this agitation, he told the protectorate's second parliament that unless an alternative form of public maintenance of the ministry were first settled, the removal of tithes would be an injustice he could not possibly countenance.[37]

In 1659 Milton took up the problems of toleration and tithes in two pamphlets issued in February and August, which contained his

[37] Woolrych's introduction to CPW, vol. VII, contains a discussion of Cromwell's ecclesiastical policy and Milton's attitude, pp. 27–33; for Cromwell's statement on tithes in his speech of 1656, see W. C. Abbott, *The Writings And Speeches of Oliver Cromwell*, 4 vols. (Cambridge, Mass.: Harvard University Press, 1937–1947), vol. IV, p. 272.

most heartfelt sentiments on the subject. The first, *A Treatise of Civil Power in Ecclesiastical Causes*, appeared before the protectorate's demise and was addressed to Richard Cromwell's parliament. The second, *Considerations Touching The Likeliest Means to Remove Hirelings Out of The Church*, appeared after the recall of the Rump, to which it was dedicated. Both centered on religious liberty, the first in its relation to the civil power, the second in its relation to the payment of ministers. The latter of these tracts indicated in passing that Milton had recanted his earlier adherence to the protectorate. Hailing the Rump's members as "the authors and best patrons of religious and civil libertie, that ever these Ilands brought forth," he voiced his gratitude for their reinstatement by a miraculous providence "after a short but scandalous night of interruption." This last phrase clearly implied that he no longer approved of Cromwell's and the army's expulsion of the Long Parliament which he had formerly defended, although an intermission of six years was hardly a short period.[38]

His two pamphlets were an uncompromising statement in the name of Christian liberty against state control of religion and compulsory tithes, twin evils which he execrated as the root of all religious tyranny and corruption. *A Treatise of Civil Power* contended that the magistrate possessed no rightful authority over conscience or the church. Since, as all Protestants agreed, Scripture was the sole rule of faith, there could be no infallible judge as to its meaning. Certainly neither the state nor church was such a judge. Hence the individual should be left free to understand it according to his own conscience, which must remain immune from force or coercion. He dismissed apprehensions about the danger of heresy, blasphemy, and the spread of error as groundless fears. Scripture carried its own self–evidence as the word of God, and religion could derive no hurt from the opinions of any who based their faith on seeking its guidance with the help of the holy spirit. Catholics, he suggested, were the only true heretics, because they alone clung to traditions and beliefs not probable by Scripture. He denied that Paul's teaching on the duty of obedience in the letter to the Romans gave the state any power over the church. Only Christ had the government of the church, a spiritual kingdom with purely spiritual weapons to which the magistrate's authority did not extend. He accused Protestants of

---

[38] *Considerations Touching The Likeliest Means to Remove Hirelings Out of The Church,* CPW, vol. VII, p. 274; see Woolrych's discussion of the meaning of this passage, ibid., pp. 85–86, and in "Milton And Cromwell: 'A Short But Scandalous Night of Interruption'," *Achievements of The Left Hand,* ed. Michael Lieb and John T. Shawcross (Amherst: University of Massachusetts Press, 1974).

betraying their own principles when they oppressed others who relied on Scripture in the formation of their beliefs. How much persecution, cruelty, and bloodshed, he lamented, had Protestants caused by their failure to distinguish correctly between civil and ecclesiastical power. All these arguments added up to the conclusion that the civil power's resort to compulsion in religion not only did no good but violated the Christian liberty of all believers, whose consciences the gospel had freed from every form of bondage.[39]

Milton's treatise on civil power passed largely unnoticed. His view represented an extreme position that few of his contemporaries shared. Beside doing away with an established church, he would also have deprived the state of any authority in matters of religion. This was a drastic and probably impractical step to propose in a society in which religion and church affiliation were major influences on individual and collective conduct. Even among strong advocates of toleration, most were willing to accept some type of a public establishment of religion and allow the state a role in the supervision of religious life provided it permitted freedom of conscience and worship to dissenters. Milton was also guilty of considerable epistemological question-begging in opposing toleration for Catholics. Why wasn't the Catholic conscience as much entitled to freedom as the Protestant? If there could be no infallible judge of the conscience of Protestants in their interpretation of Scripture, how could there be one that pronounced the consciences of Catholics in error when they looked to the church as well as to Scripture as the source of truth? It was absurd for him to assert, as he did, that Catholicism was not really a religion, but a Roman papal attempt at universal dominion.[40] He also called it a heresy against Scripture and said that the conscience of Catholics was enthralled to man instead of God;[41] but this only made a dogma of the Protestant principle and implicitly assumed infallibility to himself in defining heresy. Had he wished to refuse toleration to Catholics on strictly political grounds, it would have been more consistent to concede liberty to those who remained peaceable and refrained from using their religion as an excuse for plotting against the state.

Considerations Touching The Likeliest Means to Remove Hirelings Out of The Church was equally extreme in urging the total disendowment of the church by abolishing tithes and other required payments to

---

[39] *A Treatise of Civil Power*, pp. 242, 243, 244, 246, 247, 248–249, 252, 253, 262, 265.

[40] Ibid., p. 254.

[41] Ibid., p. 254.

ministers. The restored Rump had received many petitions from sectarians and others for the removal of such charges, and Milton's purpose was to support these demands, which some of the army's leaders likewise endorsed. He began his argument by stressing his own claim to be heard as the man whose reason and ability had successfully defended the cause of the commonwealth to all nations. By "hirelings" he meant those who entered the ministry for mercenary reasons. In his mind these were the majority, and his call to parliament to deliver the nation from the "oppressions of a Simonious and decimating clergie" contained a strong undertone of contempt and dislike of the clerical order. Once again he invoked Christian liberty as the ground for ending the compulsory support of ministers. Although God had allowed tithes to the Levites under the ceremonial law of the Old Testament, the new dispensation of the gospel, which superseded the old law, left the church to charity and the Christian freedom of people to give or not as they thought good. He inveighed against the extortion of the Presbyterian and other clergy who demanded tithes by law, sued their parishioners, and tried to persuade a Christian magistracy that they had a right to these payments. The exaction of fees for christenings, marriages, and burials likewise fell under his ban. In this connection he reiterated the opinion in his divorce tracts that according to Scripture, marriage was purely a "civil ordinance" or "household contract" requiring no involvement by the clergy. He felt sure that if all compulsory payments ceased, hirelings would no longer be lured by "these tempting baits" into the church. In their place, he would have had ministers serve gratis or maintain themselves either by voluntary offerings or their own labor. If one community was too poor to support a minister by its contributions, it could join with others for this purpose or seek aid from the charity of rich congregations. Ministers in any case needed neither a university education nor much learning to perform their office of teaching, nor did people need them for longer than it took to learn the basic principles of religion, after which they could depend on themselves. He recommended that tithes and ministerial salaries should be used instead to erect schools and libraries throughout the land which could teach languages and arts and exercise a civilizing effect on the people. Those trained by these institutions could then become local preachers, giving their services freely in recompense for what they had freely received. He denied the magistrate any power to determine the fitness of ministers and was completely opposed to government support of the clergy from public taxation, an arrangement he considered inconsistent "with the people's right" and "Christian liberty." The civil magistrate possessed authority only over civil matters and could not compel a person against his conscience to give for the support of a religion.[42]

Milton's religious idealism was manifest in his desire to protect the Christian conscience from any form of compulsion in order to assure that everything relating to faith would be free and voluntary. So great was the responsibility he placed on the individual believer, and so little did he take account of the corporate life of religion, that he virtually dispensed with the necessity of a professional ministry. His proposed remedy of ending tithes without providing any substitute ignored all the historical, legal, and human complications of the intricate question of ministerial support. It is difficult to see how the legislature could have accepted it. The parish clergy had a property interest in tithes; if deprived of them, they were surely entitled to compensation. Beyond that, how were men who had perhaps spent years in the ministry to maintain themselves and their families if all obligatory payments ceased? Carried away by his animosity, Milton ignored all these difficulties. He would simply have cut through them by the surgery of abolition. As his foremost biographer rightly commented,

> It is not with a flesh-and-blood world that he deals, a world of men, and their wives, and their families, and their yearly incomes, and household belongings. It is with a world of wax, or of flesh and blood that must be content to be treated as wax.[43]

There can be little doubt that Milton's *Treatise of Civil Power* and his subsequent jubilation at the recall of the Rump signified a reversal of his attitude toward the protectorate. While his admiration for Cromwell as a great leader probably remained intact, his misgivings must have grown not only about the Lord Protector's retention of tithes and state authority over the church, but about the investment of power in a single person and the preponderant role of the army. Some of his friends may even have wondered about his *bona fides*

---

[42] *Considerations Touching The Likeliest Means*, pp. 275, 278, 281, 295, 297, 299, 300, 301–304, 305, 306, 307, 315, 317. It is worth noting that in August 1653 the Nominated Parliament convened by the army after the expulsion of the Rump (see above, p. 91) passed an ordinance establishing civil marriage and providing that only a marriage performed before a Justice of the Peace would be recognized by the state; see S. R. Gardiner, *History of the Commonwealth and Protectorate*, 4 vols. (London: Longmans, Green, 1903), vol. II, p. 292.

[43] David Masson, *The Life of John Milton in Connexion with The Political, Ecclesiastical, And Literary History of His Time*, 7 vols. (London, 1859–1894), vol. V, p. 615.

when he continued in employment under the protectorate. What did Bradshaw and Vane, for example, statesmen he esteemed who condemned Cromwell's rule, think of him then? A letter from a republican friend in May 1659 seems to show that he had been somewhat suspect, The writer frankly stated his uncertainty whether Milton's relationship to the Cromwellian court "had not clouded your former Light," until the appearance of *A Treatise of Civil Power* had resolved his doubt.[44] Republicanism, nevertheless, was still the heart of Milton's political creed. After the fall of the protectorate he gave renewed expression to it in a last attempt to preserve the expiring revolution.

Rather than a prelude to stability, the Rump's reinstatement in May proved merely a stop-gap. Exerting a high hand in order to reassert parliamentary control of the army, the Rump's republican leaders angered the senior military officers, who strongly resented its policies and desired independent power for themselves. In October, after suppressing a small Royalist rising, they expelled the Rump for a second time. History seemed to be repeating itself as farce. The officers tried to govern on their own through a committee of safety, but met widespread criticism, refusals to pay taxes, and calls for a free parliament. Meanwhile, both they and the army itself were becoming ever more disunited. The commander of the English forces stationed in Scotland, General George Monck, supported by his own troops and some of those around London, let it be known that he favored the submission of military to civil authority. At the end of December, the rebellious officers, bankrupt for an alternative, recalled the Rump once more. Immediately thereafter Monck marched his army to England. Arriving in London in February 1660, he became the inscrutable arbiter of all affairs. While he concealed his intentions, multitudes called on him to act to procure a free parliament. The Rump, failing to take measures to fill up vacancies in the House of Commons or to proceed toward its dissolution, had few supporters and was in a very weak position. In London the city government and populace expressed strong opposition to its existence. Both its leaders and many of the army's officers feared, however, that elections to a new parliament, unless highly restricted, would open the floodgates to royalism and put finis to the republic.

Perceiving the broad resistance to its continuance, Monck finally threw his weight against the Rump. At the end of February, under his protection, more than ninety secluded members, specters out of

[44] Letter from Moses Wall, CPW, vol. VII, pp. 510–511. Little is known about Wall, who was a republican, religious radical, and ardent social reformer.

the past whom the army had purged eleven years before, were readmitted to their seats in parliament. With the republicans now outnumbered, the reconstituted assembly within a period of two weeks voted new taxes to pay the army, annulled the Rump's former engagement promising fidelity to a commonwealth without a king or house of lords, named a new Council of State, and decreed its own dissolution on 16 March after providing for the election of a new free parliament to meet in the following month. With this decision the revolutionary Long Parliament that had first met in 1640 finally came to an end. By now a massive body of opinion reflecting all sections of society had apparently reached the conclusion that only the return of kingship could put a stop to political confusion and uncertainty, and the stage was set for a royal restoration.[45]

Milton performed his last tasks for the Council of State in May 1659, although his formal employment did not cease for another few months. Watching events from the sidelines, he felt great alarm that his country was hastening back to its former servitude. At stake was the survival of what by 1659 was widely known as the Good Old Cause. This phrase, which became current in the final years of the revolution, signified loyalty to the twin principles of religious toleration and civil liberty embodied in republican government. By the later 1650s republicanism had gained a considerable following on the political scene. The demise of kingship created a conceptual space for the pursuit of new political alternatives that looked for inspiration to the constitutions of the republics of antiquity and modern Venice. Among the politicians and writers who helped create a political culture of republicanism at this moment were Sir Henry Vane the younger, Thomas Chaloner, Marchamont Nedham, Henry Neville, Algernon Sidney, and James Harrington.[46] Neville's *Plato Redivivus*

[45] The events leading up to the Restoration are surveyed in Woolrych's introduction to CPW, vol VII, and recounted in detail in Godfrey Davies, *The Restoration of Charles II* (San Marino, Calif.: The Huntington Library, 1955) and Ronald Hutton, *The Restoration* (New York: Oxford University Press, 1987), chaps. 1–5.

[46] On these men and the republicanism of the period, see Zera S. Fink, *The Classical Republicans*, (Evanston: Northwestern University Press, 1945); Perez Zagorin, *A History of Political Thought in The English Revolution* (London: Routledge & Kegan Paul, 1954), chaps. X–XII; the introduction to *The Political Works of James Harrington*, ed. J. G. Pocock (Cambridge: Cambridge University Press, 1977); Blair Worden, "Classical Republicanism And The Puritan Revolution," in *History And Imagination. Essays in Honour of H. R. Trevor-Roper*, ed. Hugh Lloyd-Jones, Valerie Pearl, Blair Worden (London: Duckworth, 1981); Jonathan Scott, *Algernon Sidney And The English Republic* (Cambridge: Cambridge University Press, 1988).

and Sidney's *Discourses on Government* were not published until long after the Restoration, but the genesis of their republican principles lay in the discussions of the interregnum when they were active political figures. Most influential of all the republican theorists of the time was James Harrington, whose utopian design for an English republic, *The Commonwealth of Oceana*, issued in 1656, attracted a large number of disciples. *Oceana* depicted an aristocratic republic governed by landed gentlemen accountable to the people. Its institutions were intended to guarantee both civil and religious liberty in a commonwealth that would last forever. They included an agrarian law limiting the amount of land anyone could own so as to prevent too great an inequality between the citizens, regular rotation in office and use of the ballot, and an elected senate and popular assembly, the first to debate laws and policy without deciding, the second to vote on them without discussion. *Oceana* also provided for a state church, but granted religious freedom to dissenters. Harrington dedicated his work to Cromwell, hoping to convert him to his views. After the fall of the protectorate, he continued his republican propaganda and his writings became the focal point of republican debate. In 1659–60, nearly everyone eager to avert the return of kingship seized on some aspect of his ideas.[47]

Milton was shocked into entering the political arena once more by the dissensions between the army and parliament, which created serious instability at the center of government and threatened to end in the destruction of everything in which he believed. In October 1659, following the army's second expulsion of the Rump, he made his earliest comment on the situation in a hastily drafted communication to a friend deploring the "dangerous ruptures of the commonwealth." To overcome the prevailing anarchy he proposed the establishment of a "senate or general Councell of State" to manage affairs. This body would consist of the parliament, should it be restored, or else be chosen by the army, which was to remain in close union with it. The conditions of its rule were to be the abjuration of monarchy and full liberty of conscience to all who based their faith on Scripture, plus the support of committees of the "faithfullest adherents" of the cause in every county. This was the first time Milton mentioned government by a specially appointed senate or council, a notion that was to obsess him in the months preceding the Restoration as the only way to preserve the commonwealth.[48]

[47] On Harrington's work and influence, see Pocock's introduction to *The Political Works of James Harrington* and the account in Zagorin, chaps. XI–XII.
[48] *A Letter to A Friend, Concerning The Ruptures of The Commonwealth*, CPW, vol.

Shortly afterward he brought up the same idea again in a brief set of unpublished proposals to avoid a civil war and attain a firm government. One of its provisions stated that parliament should be restored and its members sit for life. This was necessary, he believed, to eliminate the novelties and commotions incident to successive parliaments. Moreover, since the name "parliament" was of Norman-French derivation and hence a monument of the nation's servitude, he recommended calling the ruling body a "Grand or Supreme Counsell." Those subsequently elected to it were to be chosen by the Grand Council itself and "the well affected people." Agreement to liberty of conscience and against government by a single person and house of lords was to be the condition of membership. This institution was to name a council of state from its own number to function as its executive. Although he outlined some further particulars, these were the main expedients he deemed necessary for rescuing his country and without which, he warned, "we are like to fall into evills & discords incurable, the speedy end whereof wilbe utter ruine, which God of his mercy prevent!"[49]

By 1660 Milton retained little or no faith in regularly elected parliaments. He had come to feel that such an institution, subject to corruption, ambition, and misguided political pressures, was incapable of consistently upholding civil or religious liberty. The digression in his *History of Britain* on the character of the Long Parliament, which was probably written in 1660 around the time of the Restoration, indicates how greatly his opinion of parliament had changed. He was bitterly critical of the factionalism, oppressions, hypocrisy, and self-seeking that marked the Long Parliament's record in his eyes. Some of its members, he declared contemptuously, "calld from shops & warehouses without other merit," had simply fallen, "as thir breeding was ...to hucster the commonwealth." The parliament's failure to live up to his expectations led him to the pessimistic conclusion that in a corrupt and degenerate age the people were unfit for liberty, which could be handled only "by just and vertuous men," and

VII, pp. 324, 325, 327, 329, 330, 331. The person to whom Milton addressed this letter is unknown; it was first published in 1698.

[49] *Proposalls of Certaine Expedients for The Preventing of A Civill War Now Feard, & The Settling of A Firme Government*, CPW, vol. VII, pp. 336–338, 339. Milton wrote this document between late October and late December 1659, prior to the army's second restoration of the Rump; it was not published until the twentieth century; see the preface of the editor, Maurice Kelley, p. 334.

was unsuitable to the bad and dissolute who needed rather to be curbed.[50]

Deeply concerned over the quarrels and disunion among the adherents of the Good Old Cause, he sought desperately for ways to prop up the failing commonwealth. His certainty that a free parliamentary election must inevitably result in the return of monarchy forced him to limit even further his original belief in popular sovereignty and consent as the root of government. In a letter of advice of February or March 1660 apparently intended for General Monck, he predicted that unless elections to a new parliament were restricted to those firmly opposed to the rule of a single person and house of lords, "our Liberties will be utterly lost...." Urging Monck to act speedily to maintain a free commonwealth, he suggested the creation of a "Grand or General Council," chosen by rightly qualified people, which would sit perpetually as the supreme governing body and serve as the custodian of public liberty.[51]

He was by no means alone during this period of confusion in looking for some extraordinary institutional safeguard for republican freedom to prevent an elected legislature from attempting to bring back the government of a single person. The same conception was common among the adherents of the Good Old Cause. In 1659 the army's leaders submitted a list of demands to the restored Rump which included the appointment of a "select senate" composed of "able and faithful persons, eminent for godliness and such as continue adhering to this cause," which would share power with an elected House of Commons. The republican politician Edmund Ludlow proposed the naming of twenty-one "Conservators of Liberty" with the same end in mind. Sir Henry Vane the younger, in a critique of Harrington's ideas, advocated the limitation of political rights for a time exclusively to godly people well affected to the public freedom, who would choose a ruling senate or body of elders to act as a corrective or balance to an elected assembly. Another republican, Henry Stubbe, Vane's friend and follower, argued for a

---

[50] *Mr John Miltons Character of The Long Parliament*, 1681, CPW, vol. V, pt. I, pp. 443, 445, 449. On the composition and date of this digression in Milton's *History of Britain*, see above, p. 66.

[51] *The Present Means, And Brief Delineation of A Free Commonwealth, Easy to Put in Practice, And without Delay, in A Letter to General Monck*, 1660, CPW, vol. VII, pp. 393–394. This document seems to have been written soon after Monck restored the secluded members of 1648 to their seats in the Long Parliament. Milton had in view the arrangements the latter was making for elections to a new parliament prior to its dissolution; see the introduction by the editor, Robert W. Ayers, pp. 388–391.

"Select Senate, or Conservators of the liberties of England," whose members would sit for life to act as a check on parliaments.[52]

The defenders of the Good Old Cause confronted the same problem that weighed on all the successive regimes of the interregnum: how to reconcile their professed commitment to political rights and popular sovereignty with the fact that the majority of the political nation, if free to choose, would opt for a return to monarchy. Milton proffered his solution to this dilemma in his final plea for a republic, *The Readie And Easie Way to Establish A Free Commonwealth*, a pamphlet undertaken in a last vain hope of arresting the headlong rush back to Stuart rule. Published in late February 1660, a second larger edition followed in April, less than two months before the restoration of Charles II. In exposing his anti-monarchical opinions so outspokenly at such a moment he stood virtually alone. He took a big risk in doing so, but the political fearlessness he evinced in the past was more evident now than ever. Moreover, as the man proud of winning European fame for his defense of the English republic, he felt it his duty to try to save it from impending ruin.[53]

Milton justified parliament's abolition of kingship in 1649 as done in accord with the law of nature, "the only law of laws truly and properly to all mankinde fundamental", and "the beginning an end of all Government...." He went on to paint a grim picture of the consequences of a restoration beside the loss of freedom: the heavy taxes, fines, and impositions to be expected; the confusion and danger to estates; the revenge certain to be visited on untold numbers; the return of episcopacy, inseparably united in interest

---

[52] On these proposals, see Davies, pp. 98, 186; Woolrych's introduction, pp. 72–73, 104–106, 126–128; Zagorin, pp. 161–162. Ludlow described his plan for conservators of liberty in his *Memoirs*, ed. C. H. Firth, 2 vols. (Oxford, 1894), vol. II, p. 172; Vane presented his scheme in his anonymously published tract, *A Needful Corrective or Ballance in Popular Government*, 1659, which is discussed by Margaret Judson, *The Political Thought of Sir Henry Vane* (Philadelphia: University of Pennsylvania Press, 1969), pp. 39–40; Stubbe outlined his conception in *A Letter to An Officer of The Army Concerning A Select Senate*, 1659. Barbara K. Lewalski has discussed Milton's views in 1659–60 in the context of other republican writings and the political situation in "Milton: Political Beliefs And Polemical Methods, 1659–1660," *Publications of The Modern Language Association*, vol. LXXIV, no. 1 (1959).

[53] *The Readie And Easie Way to Establish A Free Commonwealth*, 2nd ed., 1660, CPW, vol. VII, pp. 420. This volume also prints the first edition. The preface by the editor, Robert W. Ayers, discusses the differences between the two editions, which were mainly the result of adaptations to changing events. My account is based on the second edition.

with kingship. As for the "new royaliz'd presbyterians," he warned that they would not be forgiven their earlier actions against monarchy despite having recanted what they had done. He felt contempt and shame that the nation, heedless of its honor and God's favors, could "creep back so poorly as it seems the multitude would to thir once abjur'd and detested thraldom of kingship...." If the people did this, they would slander their own just and religious deeds to become the scorn and derision of the world. They would soon repent of their decision, moreover, when they experienced anew the royal encroachments on their conscience and found themselves forced to fight another civil war to recover their lost freedom. He lauded the virtues of a free commonwealth as the form of government closest to the teachings of Christ. In a republic even the greatest men were servants of the people, living in equality with their fellows, and friendly and accessible to all. A king, on the other hand, needed to be adored like a god. The cause of vast expense and luxury, he was surrounded by a dissolute and haughty court which debauched the prime gentry of both sexes and produced a servile nobility intent on court office instead of public service. Milton was sure that the government of a free, elected council ruled by reason provided the best guarantee of the nation's happiness. He could not understand why a people able to manage their own affairs should want to devolve power upon one person who would be their lord, not servant. Having fought so gloriously for liberty, if the English and their leaders now renounced the fruit of their victory over tyranny, their ignominy would exceed any that ever befell a free nation. They would deserve to be slaves, although a worthier part of the nation would refuse to follow them into bondage.[54]

After these strictures he proceeded to outline the form of a free and enduring commonwealth, which he imagined could be established promptly and easily by the new parliament summoned to meet later in April. Its main institution would be a grand or general council or senate chosen by the people to sit perpetually. This council would possess sovereignty, "not transferred, but delegated only, and as it were deposited...." Noting the evil effects of successive parliaments, he proposed to abolish even the name of parliament as a relic of the Norman Conquest. He was well aware of Harrington's writings, although he never mentioned him by name. As a reluctant concession to Harrington's followers, and in case a lifetime council seemed to block some men's ambition or entail too absolute a power, he was willing to consider a rotating membership on the council, with a

[54] Ibid., pp. 412–413, 422, 423, 425, 427, 428, 450–451.

certain number of members replacing others at intervals. But as rotation was likely to thrust out the best and ablest men, he preferred to avoid it if possible. The members should thus be permanent and removeable only by death or for criminal misconduct. He found precedents for this supreme body in the institutions of other free commonwealths: the Jewish Sanhedrin, the Athenian Areopagus and Spartan elders, the senates of Rome and Venice, and the provincial estates of the Dutch republic, which all consisted of life members. Without a perpetual council, he was firmly convinced, a commonwealth would neither be well ordered nor able to provide for its safety.[55]

He gave a vague sketch of the procedure for electing the council's members. Only rightly qualified persons would be eligible to vote. These would first meet to nominate as many candidates as they liked; then the latter would meet to nominate others "of a better breeding." After several such siftings, a select number would remain from which a majority would choose the worthiest. The aim of these arrangements was "to make the people fittest to chuse and the chosen fittest to governe," to inculcate virtue and justice, and to teach everyone to identify their private welfare and happiness with "the public peace, libertie, and safetie." If this were achieved, there would be no reason to mistrust the patriots elected to the Grand Council, who would be true keepers of liberty.[56]

He criticized Harrington's proposed republic as unwieldy and exotic, arguing that its innovations would simply "manacle the native liberty of mankinde" and endanger property by its agrarian law. His own plan seemed to him easy to implement and capable of making his country the freest in the world. To the objection that far the greater part of the nation wanted a return to kingship, he replied that the minority was not obliged to submit to the majority's desire. This greater part had "lost the right of ...election" both in reason and by its defeat in the war. It was more just that the lesser number compel the greater to retain their liberty than that the greater number should force the lesser "to be thir fellow slaves." "Those who seek nothing but thir own just libertie," he claimed, "have alwaies right to winn it and to keep it, when ever they have power, be the voices never so numerous that oppose it."[57]

The Readie And Easie Way's second edition had relatively little to say about religion. Its chief point was that a free commonwealth

[55] Ibid., pp. 430–437, 444.
[56] Ibid., pp. 442–443.
[57] Ibid., pp. 444–446, 455.

would be most favorable to liberty of conscience as an essential part of human liberty. Civil liberty itself Milton also connected with a large degree of decentralization and local autonomy. To this end he proposed that every county should become a little commonwealth, possessing its own local assembly to make laws and communicate its views to the General Council. In these county communities a resident nobility would take the leading part in affairs and local courts would administer justice. Schools and academies would also be widely established to give children an education in liberal arts and spread religion, knowledge, and civility throughout the land. Amidst all these particulars, Milton was always intent on his republican ideal. While a free commonwealth aimed to make the people "flourishing, vertuous, noble and high-spirited," he said, monarchies sought to make them soft, base, vicious, and servile so that they could be more easily kept under. To reassure against the fear that a perpetual council might grow corrupt, he pointed out that the commonwealth would consist of many commonwealths united into one entrusted sovereignty; it would have a faithful army or settled militia, its accounts would be open to public inspection, its laws and taxes determined by vote, and no distinction would exist between lords and commoners of a kind that could divide the public interest. Hence there would be no way for the supreme council to become corrupt or invade liberty. Yet if these securities did not suffice to allay concern, he reiterated his readiness to include rotation of membership as a further safeguard.[58]

In summing up, he struck a deeply pessimistic note. That "a few and easie things, now seasonably don," could save his country, he professed not to doubt. Yet he admitted that if the people were so set as to prostitute religion and liberty to bring back kingship, then the nation's condition was rotten and it would fall back into slavery by God's judgment. Nevertheless, he had done his duty, he said, to try to forewarn his country in time, speaking "the language of that which is not call'd amiss the good Old Cause...." Although recognizing that he might have uttered "the last words of expiring libertie," he hoped he had spoken persuasion to sensible men and that God would raise up some to become "children of reviving libertie." In his last foreboding sentences against "chusing a captain back to Egypt," he bemoaned the "epidemic madness" that was carrying England to destruction "through the general defection of a misguided and abus'd multitude."[59]

Faced with the prospect of the commonwealth's imminent

58 Ibid., pp. 456–457, 458–460, 461.
59 Ibid., pp. 461–463.

extinction, Milton put his whole heart into his plea for a republic. His wide learning in ancient and modern history made him believe that this was the highest type of government producing the highest type of character. Numerous echoes of the republicanism of classical antiquity, its pride in the freedom of collective self-rule and its antipathy to the domination of a single person, whether king or tyrant, were audible in his pages.[60] In fixing on a perpetual council or senate as the fundamental institution of government in his proposed polity, he gave full rein to the principle of aristocratic virtue that informed his republican ideal. His aim was to assure the rule of the worthiest, those who came up to his own standard of self-command and fidelity to the public good. Individual rights counted for little in comparison with this most desirable end. He no longer trusted in the people or elected parliaments. The first had become in his mind the inconsiderate and misguided multitude, the second a cause of unsettlement, commotions, and novelty.[61] While still loyal to the abstract doctrine of popular sovereignty, he gave the people no function in his commonwealth except the passive role of accepting the guidance of their virtuous governors.

His proposal to banish the name and being of parliament in favor of a perpetual supreme council was not only impracticable, but showed little understanding of the political situation. The English were far too strongly attached to parliaments as part of their ancient constitution to find such an idea tolerable; much less would the next parliament do so, to which he appealed to put his model into effect. After the Long Parliament's lengthy tenure, the Rump's dependence on the army, and its refusal to make way for a successor, the strongest demand of the political nation and many others was for a freely elected parliament. This was part of their conception of English liberty. That such a parliament was likely to restore the king only added to its attraction.

To prevent a royal restoration, Milton limited the suffrage in his commonwealth to those rightly qualified, frankly declaring that the majority of the people had lost the right of election. This would have excluded not only old Royalists but Presbyterians and many others who, for whatever reason, opposed the Good Old Cause. There was also a social bias in his polity, which incorporated deference to worldly rank. The electors and those who sat in the General Council

---

[60] Fink, chap. 4, discusses the influence of ancient republicanism and classical precedents on *The Readie And Easie Way* and Milton's earlier writings, but exaggerates the importance of the theory of the mixed state in his thinking.

[61] Ibid., pp. 434–436.

were to be persons of "better breeding", while members of the nobility held primacy in local government. Equally frankly, he maintained that the virtuous minority could justly compel the servile majority to submit to a republic. This meant endorsing the minority's coercion of the majority for as long as necessary; and, indeed, probably in no other way could a restoration have been prevented in 1660. Such a situation, however, was clearly untenable. To preserve liberty, Milton was willing to suppress it, depriving those who rejected his republican prescription of the right of citizenship. His reasoning explains the defeat of the Good Old Cause. Conscious of being greatly outnumbered, discredited by its political failures and internal dissensions, its supporters could stay in power only by force and resistance to the national will.

At about the same time as the publication of *The Readie And Easie Way*'s second edition, Milton uttered one other word in the face of the advancing tide. Incensed by a Royalist clergyman's printed sermon on the text, "My son, fear God and the king," (Proverbs 24:21), he issued a scathing reply. Here he affirmed that monarchy in England had been abolished by the right of conquest and in accord with the law of nature, which entitled every free to people to choose their government. Again he defended the superiority of a free commonwealth as the best polity "for civil, virtuous and industrious nations...." His despondency was evident, nevertheless, in the remark that if the nation was determined to have a king, then it should choose someone "out of our own number...who hath best aided the people, and best merited against tyrannie...." By this despairing alternative he probably referred to General Monck. There was not the slightest chance, though, that Monck, one of the main architects of the Restoration, would have agreed to this suggestion.[62]

A few short weeks culminated in the event that Milton dreaded. The Convention Parliament assembled on 25 April 1660. The long missing House of Lords was back in its place and the elections to the House of Commons had returned a far larger number of Royalists and Presbyterians than republicans. Some while before, having decided that only a restoration could provide a barrier against anarchy, General Monck had opened secret communications with the exiled Charles II in the Dutch republic. On 1 May the two Houses received from Charles the Declaration of Breda, which appealed for unity and offered a pardon for all past actions and offenses, liberty to

---

[62] *Brief Notes upon a Late Sermon, Titl'd The Fear of God And The King*, 1660, CPW, vol. VII, pp. 479, 481–482.

tender consciences, confirmation of land sales and purchases made during the revolution, and payment of arrears to the army. The exact terms of all these concessions were to be defined by a free parliament, to whose legislation for the purpose Charles promised his assent. Responding warmly, the Houses voted that according to the ancient and fundamental law, the government is and ought to be in a king, lords, and commons. On 8 May Charles II was proclaimed king. A parliamentary delegation went to the Hague to escort him home, and on the 25th he arrived at Dover. Four days later he entered London to a rapturous reception from cheering masses.[63]

These changes took place with almost effortless ease and without any resistance. Contrary to the hopes of its Presbyterian members, the Convention Parliament failed to impose any prior conditions on the king as the price of his reinstatement. His reign was officially reckoned as beginning on 30 January 1649, the day of his father's execution. The acts and ordinances passed during the civil war and interregnum without royal assent became null and void. The majority of the nation welcomed the restoration of kingship with intense relief because it also meant the restoration of a free parliament and the end of military rule and republican usurpation. Its enemies did not conquer the English revolution. It died by its own hand, a victim of the disunity and weakness of those who wanted its survival. It was a sorry ending to the great struggle begun twenty years before. In 1649 Milton had written that the kings of this world

> have both ever hated, and instinctively fear'd the Church of God.
> Whether it be for that thir Doctrin seems much to favour two things
> to them so dreadful, Liberty and Equality, or because they are the
> Children of that Kingdom which, as ancient Prophesies have foretold,
> shall in the end break to peeces and dissolve all thir great power and
> Dominion.[64]

In 1660 these words turned to ashes. The profane kingdom came back in triumph and the poet was forced to ponder, in an alien political world, the meaning of God's heavy judgment on the Good Old Cause.

---

[63] Besides Davies' narrative, J. R. Jones, *Country And Court: England 1658–1714* (Cambridge, Mass.: Harvard University Press, 1978), chap. 6, and Hutton, chaps. 4–5, contain detailed accounts of the Restoration, its reasons, and the political circumstances of 1659–60 that brought it about.

[64] *Eikonoklastes*, CPW, vol. III, p. 509.

Chapter 5

AFTER THE REVOLUTION:
THE POLITICS OF THE LATER POEMS
AND MILTON'S THEODICY

For Milton the Restoration was a personal and political calamity. Beside being forced to observe the humiliating spectacle of the nation's defection as it prostrated itself before the golden calf of monarchy, his life was in danger as a notorious apologist for regicide. In May 1660 he went into hiding at a friend's house in Bartholomew Close, where he remained sequestered while the Convention Parliament debated the terms of an act of indemnity and pardon and decided on the names of those to be excepted from it by death or other penalty. On 16 June his name and that of John Goodwin, another prominent publicist for regicide, were brought up in the House of Commons. Although the House ordered the seizure and burning of all copies of Milton's *Eikonoklastes* and *Defence of The English People* and Goodwin's *The Obstructours of Justice*, as well as the arrest of the authors, neither man was proposed for execution.[1] When finally passed and assented to by the king on 19 August, the Act of Indemnity did not include Milton in any of the excepted categories. He probably owed his escape to the protection of a few influential men in parliament and the king's council who were well-disposed toward him despite his political record. This did not mean, though, that his troubles were over. In September copies of his two condemned books were publicly burned in London and Westminster by the hand of the common hangman. Sometime afterward he was arrested pursuant to the earlier order of the House of Commons. Held in prison for

---

[1] Like Milton, Goodwin, an Independent minister, was one of the first writers to defend Charles I's execution and the people's right to depose kings; see Perez Zagorin, *A History of Political Thought in The English Revolution* (London: Routledge & Kegan Paul, 1954), chap. VI. He was later excepted from the Act of Indemnity and perpetually incapacitated from holding any public office.

several weeks, he was released on 15 December after pleading the benefit of the Act of Indemnity.[2]

Even though he no longer needed to fear for his own security, he must have been deeply shaken by the punishment meted out to the regicides. During the following months eleven of them were executed as traitors. On 30 January 1661, the anniversary of Charles I's death, the bodies of Cromwell, Bradshaw, and Henry Ireton, Cromwell's son-in-law, were exhumed and gibbeted at Tyburn. Twenty other dead regicides had their lands and other property made liable to forfeiture. Of those still living, most were subjected to heavy penalties short of death. Milton's friend, Sir Henry Vane, after first being sentenced to life imprisonment, was executed in 1662, despite his having taken no part in the king's trial.[3]

Beyond these dire events, Milton witnessed the confirmation of his worst fears concerning the consequences of a royal restoration. The ultra-loyalist Cavalier Parliament, which met in May 1661 as the Convention Parliament's successor, initiated a wholesale reaction in church and state. Along with legislation to strengthen the powers of the crown, it inaugurated a renewed era of religious persecution. It restored episcopacy, reinstated the Church of England in its ecclesiastical monopoly, and returned the bishops to their former seats as members of the House of Lords. In August 1662 nearly two thousand ministers, mainly Presbyterians, who had been installed in ecclesiastical livings during the revolutionary period, were ejected from the church for refusal to conform to the worship prescribed in the Anglican prayer book, Instead of the comprehension they had hoped to find within a broadened national religious establishment, they were driven out. A series of statutes passed between 1661 and 1665 also imposed stringent penalties and disabilities on all Protestant dissenters from the state church.

During this period Milton apparently lived a retired life to avoid public notice. Although he suffered considerable financial losses as the result of the Restoration, he was still left with sufficient means to maintain his independence. He changed residences several times, finally settling in 1663 in a house in Artillery Walk. In the same year he married again, taking Elizabeth Minshull, a young woman of

[2] See David Masson, *The Life of John Milton, Narrated in Connexion with The Political, Ecclesiastical, And Literary History of His time,* 7 vols. (London, 1859–1894), vol. VI, chap. 2, and Parker, vol. I, chap. 13, for Milton's danger and escape in 1660.

[3] For details of the Act of Indemnity and the fate of the regicides, see Masson, vol. VI, pp. 54–56, and Mark Noble, *The Lives of The Regicides,* 2 vols. (London, 1798), vol. I, Introduction.

twenty-three, as his third wife to help him with his three motherless daughters. For the remainder of his life he wrote nothing on current affairs except for a pamphlet in 1673 against popery and in favor of liberty of conscience. The other prose works published in his lifetime, which included his *History of Britain,* a treatise on logic, and a Latin grammar, were all remote from contemporary political issues. Outwardly, at least, he detached himself from further political controversy. Considering his earlier reputation, it would have been highly imprudent for him to write about politics, whether he was inclined to do so or not. In any case, the censorship reimposed during the Restoration made it impossible to express his thoughts freely.

The Restoration was not merely a major crisis in Milton's life. It also made an internal exile of him. Although he had a loyal circle of friends and was by no means isolated in his personal circumstances, he felt an estrangement from the world of Restoration England. To a German acquaintance he declared in 1666 in his sole surviving letter of this period that the virtue of loyalty to his country, "After captivating me with her fair-sounding name, has almost left me without a country...."[4] Like many later political intellectuals whose hopes were shattered in the experience of revolution, he was forced to reexamine his beliefs and the positions he had held in previous years. In the earlier 1640s apocalyptic enthusiasm for reformation had carried him away in the belief that God was leading his country to overcome the fallen order of history in a breakthrough to a new and higher level of living. He had perceived the revolt against the king and church as opening a new era of religious and moral regeneration. In the great struggle for emancipation which was at hand, God had chosen the English people to show the way. More and more, however, this vision faded in the following years until it proved a delusion. After the Restoration he could not escape asking the meaning of the revolution's failure. Why did God permit its enemies to triumph and what was the reason for its defeat? Most of all, he had to make a reckoning with his former hopes and ideals and consider what remained.

The results of such reflection and reassessment lie embedded in the three great poems, *Paradise Lost, Paradise Regained*, and *Samson Agonistes*, which Milton published after the Restoration. In them we may discern the beliefs and values that sustained him following the disastrous collapse of the Good Old Cause. They should allow us to see the degree to which the convictions he held during the revolution

---

[4] This comes from a Latin letter to Peter Heimbach, printed in English translation in CPW, vol. VIII, pp. 3–4. I have preferred the version in Parker, vol. I, p. 509.

survived its defeat. Obviously, none of these poems is centrally about politics, although in touching upon many of the deepest questions of human life, all of them include significant political references, reflections, and implications. Fundamentally, all three are moral histories. They all tell of human temptation, and two of them also of human frailty, folly, and desertion of God, leading ultimately to greater wisdom and reconciliation with God. In the largest sense, all three are theodicies and affirmations of redemption in which, by showing God's providential direction of a fallen world, Milton sublimated and transcended the shock and distress of the revolution's failure.

Milton probably began the composition of *Paradise Lost* around 1658. The first edition was published in 1667. A second edition, containing a few additions and alterations and a rearrangement of the original ten books of the poem into twelve, appeared in 1674. The work encompassed the greatest of all possible subjects: God and God's son, the Messiah; the revolt of Satan and his angels and the creation of the world and human beings; the latters' fall into sin and their expulsion from paradise; and the plan of history culminating in mankind's redemption. In *Paradise Lost* Milton realized his long-cherished aim of creating a great epic poem. Earlier in life he had intended to write an epic on British history celebrating King Arthur and his heroes. The failure of the English revolution probably made this scheme impossible for him. He turned instead to a vast religious subject, one of the literary projects he had also previously considered, in order, as he said in his invocation at the beginning of *Paradise Lost*, to "assert eternal providence, and justify the ways of God to men." (I, 25–26).[5]

From youth onward Milton was actuated by a profound belief in his own chosenness and the grandest conception of the poet's vocation as a prophet and teacher of nations. By long, intense discipline he strove to shape his life as a preparation to write of the greatest things in immortal verse. Despite the frustration and disappointment of his experience as a political partisan, they never caused him to lessen his poetic ambition nor to doubt his prophetic vocation. In undertaking an epic poem, he chose what Renaissance literary criticism considered the highest and most difficult of all

[5] For details on the composition and publication of *Paradise Lost* and the precursor of its theme among Milton's earlier literary projects, see CF, pp. 419–426, and J. H. Hanford and J. G. Taafe, *A Milton Handbook*, 5th ed. (New York: Meredith Corporation, 1970), pp. 147–161.

poetic forms, one dealing with the greatest actions and demanding encyclopedic knowledge and the mightiest creative powers. The invocation to book one of *Paradise Lost* states that the poet intends to pursue "Things unattempted yet in prose or rhyme," and implores the Spirit's help so that he may rise to the height of his "great argument." (I, 16, 24). Here as well as in the poem's other invocations at the beginning of the third, seventh, and ninth books, in which he prays for divine guidance and aid, he leaves no doubt that his petitions have been answered. Hence his work assumes the character of an inspired voice speaking divine truths.

The invocations also contain allusions to the author's isolation because of his blindness and the hostility by which he felt himself encompassed during the Restoration, while also expressing continued assurance in his own powers:

> More safe I sing with mortal voice, unchanged
> To hoarse or mute, though fallen on evil days,
> On evil days though fallen, and evil tongues;
> In darkness, and with dangers compassed round,
> And solitude.... (VII, 24–28)

With keen pathos he laments his loss of sight:

> Thus with the year
> Seasons return, but not to me returns
> Day, or the sweet approach of even or morn,
> Or sight of vernal bloom, or summer's rose,
> Or flocks or herds, or human face divine;
> But cloud in stead, and ever during dark
> Surrounds me, from the cheerful ways of men
> Cut off.... (III, 40–47)

Confident, though, of heavenly assistance, he knows that in his blindness he will be afforded an inner vision that sees deeper than the phenomenal world.

> So much the rather thou, celestial Light,
> Shine inward, and the mind through all her powers
> Irradiate, there plant eyes, all mist from thence
> Purge and disperse, that I may see and tell
> Of things invisible to mortal sight. (III, 51–54)

Images associated with the spiritual power of light are prominent in *Paradise Lost* and particularly characterize God the Father, the fountain of light, who sits throned amidst a glorious brightness from which even the seraphim must veil their eyes. (III, 375–382)[6] The poet's own inspiration appears as a celestial illumination that compensates for his blindness and encourages him to aspire to equal the renown of

> Blind Thamyris, and blind Maeonides,
> And Tiresias and Phineus, prophets old.   (III, 34–36)

Neither in *Paradise Lost* nor in his two later poems is there any indication that Milton ever repented or modified the earlier beliefs and principles which were basic to his political outlook. True, certain of his opinions changed markedly, and he no longer retained any faith in the regenerative value of collective revolutionary action. If some of his views altered, however, he remained consistently loyal to the root values that had underlain his previous political judgments. At no time, moreover, does he allow us to infer that he admitted error or regret concerning the positions he had formerly maintained. His biggest disappointment was in the English people, who had betrayed his hopes and in whom he had ceased to believe. This disillusionment, however, did not cause him to reproach himself for the vastly exaggerated optimism he had felt in the 1640s. If the people did not live up to his hopes for them, then this was proof not of his own unrealistic expectations but of their unworthiness and ingratitude to God for delivering them from tyranny. Likewise, he did not take his disenchantment with nearly all the revolutionary parties and the Long Parliament itself as a sign of self-deception and lack of political insight on his part; it was evidence rather of their political backsliding and corruption. In short, Milton's pride and self-conception as a prophetic poet did not allow him to think that he could have been seriously at fault in his past opinions. He did not interpret the revolution's ultimate undoing as a personal failure of political understanding or foresight. Since he was not to blame if the Good Old Cause succumbed, he accepted no share of responsibility for its collapse. Looking back on his record, it is likely that he would have compared himself with the dauntless seraph Abdiel, who challenged Satan to his face in front of an assembly of the fallen angels:

> Abdiel, faithful found
> Among the faithless, faithful only he;

[6] See Isabel G. MacCaffrey, *Paradise Lost as "Myth"* (Cambridge, Mass.: Harvard University Press, 1959), pp. 169–176, and Merritt Y. Hughes, "Milton And The Symbol of Light," in *Ten Perspectives on Milton* (New Haven: Yale University Press, 1965).

> Among innumerable false, unmoved,
> Unshaken, unseduced, unterrified
> His loyalty he kept, his love, his zeal;
> Nor number, nor example with him wrought
> To swerve from truth, or change his constant mind
> Though single.   (V, 896–903)

His identification with Abdiel in contemplating his own past seems even closer in the praise he bestows upon the loyal angel for his fortitude:

> Servant of God, well done, well hast thou fought
> The better fight, who single hast maintained
> Against revolted multitudes the cause
> Of truth, in word mightier than they in arms;
> And for the testimony of truth hast borne
> Universal reproach, far worse to bear
> Than violence: for this was all thy care
> To stand approved in sight of God, though worlds
> Judged thee perverse....   (VI, 29–37)

It is difficult to imagine that Milton did not recognize his own image in these characterizations, which resemble his stance on the eve of the Restoration in *The Readie And Easie Way*. They suggest that whatever changes of mind he may have undergone in consequence of the revolution's defeat, he was never conscious of altering his fundamental principles. Politically silenced after the Restoration, he felt sure of his own constancy amidst the apostasy and weakness of those who through fear or hope of reward yielded to the temptations of kingship.

In the civil war in heaven the rebel Milton had to be a royalist. The issues at stake in this cosmic conflict were such that he necessarily sided with God, a benevolent but absolute monarch, against the revolt of the ambitious Satan, author of evil, and his angel supporters. The task of portraying the omnipotent deity of the Bible and Christian theology presented the poet with an enormously difficult problem. Numerous critics of his treatment have noted the petty and spiteful traits in God, who leads Satan on in his futile disobedience only to inflict a terrible revenge upon him.[7] Romantic radicals like Blake and Shelley were nevertheless profoundly mistaken in imagining that because Milton endowed his Satan with outstanding qualities of leadership, courage, determination, and

---

[7] William Empson, *Milton's God*, rev. ed. (London: Chatto & Windus, 1965), contains the fullest statement of this view.

resourcefulness, he therefore unconsciously identified with him as the real hero of *Paradise Lost*.[8] The devoutly Christian poet could not have suffered from a divided mind about the devil. He had reflected long on the nature of tyranny, and his characterization presents Satan with the essential features of a dissembler and tyrant. Beside conveying a full realization of his malignity, it exposes the fraudulence of his claim to liberty.[9] Milton had witnessed many such claims during the revolution. More than once, as in the case of the Presbyterians and some of the antinomian sects, he had regarded them as no more than a pretext for license or the attainment of personal power, referring scathingly to those

> That bawl for freedom in their senseless mood
> And still revolt when truth would set them free.
> Licence they mean when they cry libertie;   (*Sonnet XII*)

His stand with a sovereign God did not involve him in inconsistency between his revolutionary past and principles and the allegiance to a

---

[8] Blake's remarks on Milton's attitude toward Satan in *The Marriage of Heaven And Hell* and Shelley's in *A Defence of Poetry* are reprinted in *Milton Criticism. Selections from Four Centuries*, ed. James Thorpe (New York: Rinehart, 1950). In his preface to *Prometheus Unbound*, however, Shelley also noted the traits of ambition, envy, revenge, and a desire for personal aggrandizement which detract from Satan's heroism; see his *Complete Poetical Works*, ed. Thomas Hutchinson (London: Oxford University Press, 1935), p. 201. The notion that Milton made Satan a heroic figure actually goes back to Dryden and was frequently stated in the eighteenth century. Many critical studies, including the classic works by E. M. W. Tillyard, *Milton* (London: Chatto & Windus, 1949), chap. 4 and passim, and C. S. Lewis, *A Preface to Paradise Lost*, rev. ed. (Oxford: Oxford University Press, 1946), pp. 89–97, have dealt with the question of Milton's conception of Satan; see also John Carey's recent discussion of the pro- and anti-Satanist positions in "Milton's Satan," *The Cambridge Companion to Milton*, ed. Dennis Danielson (Cambridge: Cambridge University Press, 1989), and the balanced and perceptive observations by Kenneth Gross, "Satan And The Romantic Satan: A Notebook," in *Re-membering Milton: Essays on Texts And Traditions*, ed. Mary Nyquist and Margaret Ferguson (London: Methuen, 1988). It is fair to say that hardly any present-day Miltonists accept the Satanist interpretation represented by Blake, Shelley, and other romantic artists.

[9] Blair Worden has implausibly argued that Milton pictured Satan as a republican and may have had Oliver Cromwell and the Puritan "saint" or hypocrite in mind as his nearest parallel; "Milton's Republicanism And The Tyranny of Heaven," in *Machiavelli And Republicanism*, ed. Gisela Bock, Quentin Skinner, Maurizio Viroli (Cambridge: Cambridge University Press, 1990, pp. 235–242. In reality, Milton makes Satan's anti-monarchical political rhetoric a screen for his ambition to attain a personal dominion in the manner of tyrants. Nowhere in Milton's later writings, moreover, is there is any indication, despite the likelihood of his disappointment with the protectorate, that he had reversed his opinion of Cromwell as a great and virtuous leader.

monarchical deity's divine power which *Paradise Lost* required. Indeed, within the constraints of the biblical story that his poem elaborated, he introduced the moral values that shaped his political ideal and made him a republican.[10]

Just as his political writings always evinced a regard for noble rank in their vision of social order, so *Paradise Lost* emphasizes the hierarchic character of celestial society, "Where honor due and reverence none neglects." (III, 607). The hosts of angels who assemble in their myriads at God's summons are distinguished into "hierarchies...orders, and degrees." (V, 591). Within the hierarchy of heaven, however, superior merit founded on virtue holds the highest place. It is made clear that the Son, whom God has seated at his right hand and named head of all the beings in heaven, is the Messiah "who by right of merit reigns." (VI, 732).[11] After he volunteers for his salvific mission of becoming man and redeeming the human race from sin by his own death, the Father pronounces him

> By merit more than birthright Son of God,
> Found worthiest to be so by being good,
> Far more than great or high;   (III, 309–311)

So compelling are the claims of virtue that the Father resigns the government of the world to the Son because of his self-sacrifice:

> Anointed universal king, all power
> I give thee, reign for ever, and assume
> Thy merits;   (III, 317–319)

The motive of Satan's rebellion, for which he was expelled from heaven with all his followers, was overweening pride and the desire "To set himself in glory above his peers," even aspiring to equality with God. (I, 39–40).[12] Envious of the Son whom God proclaimed

---

[10] Malcolm M. Ross, *Milton's Royalism. A Study of The Conflict of Symbol And Idea in The Poems* (Ithaca: Cornell University Press, 1943), argues for the opposite view that in *Paradise Lost* Milton presents conflicted conceptions and images of God's kingship and the revolt in heaven; he finds the poem's dilemma in "the conflict of royalist imagery and anti-royalist ideology...."; see p. 56 and chap. III.

[11] In her essay, "The Politics of *Paradise Lost*," in *The Politics of Discourse*, ed. Kevin Sharpe and Steven Zwicker (Berkeley: University of California Press, 1987), Mary Ann Radzinowicz stresses the crucial importance of merit rather than hereditary right in God's exaltation of the Son and also rightly notes that "Milton's meritocracy endorses hierarchy or degree.", pp. 210–211.

[12] There are Machiavellian implications in the term, "aspire," which Milton often uses to characterize Satan; see the suggestive comments by Antonio D'Andrea, "Aspiring Minds: A Machiavellian Motif from Marlowe to Milton," in *Court, Country, and Culture. Essays on Early Modern British History in Honor of Perez Zagorin,*

"Messiah and king anointed," he complains to his confederate angels that as "natives and sons of heaven," they are all

> Equally free; for orders and degrees
> Jar not with liberty, but well consist.   (V, 790–793)

By what right or reason, then, he demands to know, can the Son assume monarchy over those "in freedom equal"? (V, 794–797)

Like the controversies of the revolutionary era, this is a genuine political debate centering on the question of natural right, and the faithful Abdiel arises to refute Satan's specious argument. At the outset he rebukes Satan for his ingratitude and disobedience to the good, all-powerful creator to whom he owes his very being as well as his high station as an archangel. Satan is so puffed up with his own importance, though, that he even stupidly imagines that he is self-created and self-existent (V, 810–813, 853–859). Next, Abdiel affirms virtue's precedence over the plea for equality. While admitting it unjust "That equal over equals monarch reign," he asserts that Satan cannot count himself the equal of the Son, whom God for his merit has appointed chief of them all (V, 822–845). Despite his pretensions, Satan thus lacks the virtue of obedience and self-command which are essential to both freedom and equality. As we learn later, moreover, it is not liberty but domination that he really seeks. He thinks himself and his companions worthy

> not of liberty alone,
> Too mean pretence, but what we more affect,
> Honor, dominion, glory, and renown
> ....   (VI, 420–422)

The angel Gabriel has previously also seen his calculated toadying and exposed his insistence on liberty as a cover for his political ambition.

> And thou sly hypocrite, who now wouldst seem
> Patron of liberty, who more than thou
> Once fawned, and cringed, and servilely adored
> Heaven's awful monarch? Wherefore but in hope
> To dispossess him, and thy self to reign? (IV, 957–961)

The fallacy of Satan's attitude is exposed again when the debate resumes during the civil war in heaven. Satan now accuses the loyal

ed. Bonnelyn Young Kunze and Dwight Brautigam (Rochester: University of Rochester Press, 1992), pp. 219–221.

angels of servility (VI, 165–169), and once more it is Abdiel who replies with an even stronger affirmation of virtue's natural and divine right to rule. It is not servitude

> to serve whom God ordains
> Or nature; God and nature bid the same
> When he who rules is worthiest, and excels
> Those whom he governs. This is servitude,
> To serve the unwise, or him who hath rebelled
> Against his worthier, as thine now serve thee,
> Thy self not free, but to thy self enthralled;   (VI, 175–181)

This intensely Miltonic sentiment, derived ultimately from the fusion of Platonic and classical moral philosophy with Christian principles,[13] receives still fuller expression later, in the survey of human history after the Fall which the archangel Michael presents to Adam. More than any other part of the poem, certain of these passages contain the quintessence of Milton's enduring political philosophy, which conceives self-mastering reason and virtue as the indispensable conditions of freedom. After Michael shows the origins of kingship in Nimrod's tyrannous subjugation of his brethren, Adam understands in response that Nimrod assumed a usurped authority, since God created humans free and appointed none to be lord over another (XII, 64–71). Michael goes on to explain, however, that with the Fall men have lost true liberty, "which always with right reason dwells," because they have become prey to "inordinate desires and upstart passions" that enslave them. Having given up their inner freedom, God's just judgment often subjects them to external tyranny as well. Tyranny is therefore inevitable, "Though to the tyrant no excuse." (XII, 82–96). In the archangel's further observation on the interdependence of freedom and virtue, Milton might have been alluding to post-revolutionary England and his own countrymen:

> Yet sometimes nations will decline so low
> From virtue, which is reason, that no wrong,
> But justice, and some fatal curse annexed
> Deprives them of their outward liberty,
> Their inward lost....   (XII, 97–101)

Milton's doctrine of freedom in *Paradise Lost* constitutes an essential strand of his aristocratic republicanism and is continuous

---

[13] See Arnold Stein, *Heroic Knowledge* (Minneapolis: University of Minnesota Press, 1957), chap. 2, "The Virtues."

with the view in his earlier political writings, although possibly even more rigorous in the standard it prescribes. It is a moral doctrine that equates freedom with virtue and the rule of virtuous men. Freedom consists in striving to govern oneself in accordance with right reason. Only a people and its leaders capable of such self-government have a right to political freedom. Those enthralled within can make no claim to it; should they possess it, they will surely lose it. This lesson is reinforced in Michael's account of the times before Noah: a lesson in which the poet could also have been reflecting on the fate of the various parties of revolutionary England. Pointing to those

> First seen in acts of prowess eminent
> And great exploits, but of true virtue void; (XI, 789–790),

the archangel relates their conquests, only to foretell how conquerors and conquered alike, abandoning justice, temperance, truth, and faith, become corrupt and lose their freedom (XI, 794–807).

The biggest shift in Milton's outlook to which *Paradise Lost* bears witness is a decline in political idealism and loss of faith in the efficacy of political action and solutions. This is a typical syndrome to which many artists and intellectuals have been prone who discovered that the actualities of revolution refused to match their extravagant expectations. Following the Restoration, the poet was too disillusioned by the miscarriages of the English revolution and the victory of reaction to place much credence any longer in the prospects of historical progress or the emancipatory potentialities of the political domain. Nevertheless, this change did not cause him to subside into an apolitical quietism or indifference.[14] Instead, he rested his hopes more than ever in the spiritual growth of the individual and the ultimate overcoming of human failure and evil in history through mankind's reconciliation with God.

His deepened awareness of human limitation and weakness is most powerfully revealed in the two concluding books of *Paradise Lost*. Adam and Eve have already shown their frailty by eating the deadly

---

[14] While my view of Milton's mind after the Restoration has several features in common with the discussion of Hugh M. Richmond, *The Christian Revolutionary: John Milton* (Berkeley: University of California Press, 1974), I believe the author exaggerates his pessimism and the discontinuity between his earlier and later values and ideas. Mary Ann Radzinowicz's "The Politics of *Paradise Lost*," contains a useful corrective, as does her longer discussion of Milton's political beliefs in *Towards Samson Agonistes: The Growth of Milton's Mind* (Princeton: Princeton University Press, 1978), pt. III.

fruit in disobedience to God's command, thereby bringing death and mortal sin into the world to themselves and succeeding generations. God orders their banishment from paradise and sends the archangel Michael to tell them of his decree; but following the intercession of the Son, he bids Michael to "dismiss them not inconsolate" and "send them forth, though sorrowing, yet in peace." (XI, 113, 117). In books eleven and twelve Michael informs them of their fate, which they accept with submission, and acquaints Adam through both visions and narrative with the future that lies before their descendants. Taken from biblical history, these diverse scenes which the angel presents contain profound moral and political lessons. They constitute an important education that prepares the pair for their life in a fallen world.

From the wars of the giants who are the offspring of the daughters of men, Adam learns to comprehend the evils of war and the false glory of conquest:

> For in those days might only shall be admired,
> And valour and heroic virtue called;
> To overcome in battle and subdue
> Nations, and bring home spoils with infinite
> Manslaughter, shall be held the highest pitch
> Of human glory, and for glory done
> Of triumph, to be styled great conquerors,
> Patrons of mankind, gods, and sons of gods,
> Destroyers rightlier called and plagues of men.
> Thus fame shall be achieved, renown on earth,
> And what most merits fame in silence hid. (XI, 689–699)

He learns too, as we have previously seen, the difference between the specious "heroic virtue" based on might and true virtue consisting in self-command and obedience to right reason.

Much earlier, foreseeing the calamity of the Fall, God has promised that humanity should nevertheless find grace and that his "mercy first and last shall brightest shine." (III, 131–134). He has also promised that the race of men would at last, "by degrees of merit raised" and "under long obedience tried," find its way to blessedness,

> And earth be changed to heaven and heaven to earth,
> One kingdom, joy and union without end. (VII, 157–161)

As he reaches the final part of his unfolding of the future, Michael instructs Adam in God's plan of redemption. He tells how Jesus, conquering sin, will bring back

> Through the world's wilderness long wandered man
> Safe to eternal paradise of rest.   (XII, 310–314),

and summarizes humanity's story till the day when the earth

> Shall all be paradise, far happier place
> Than this of Eden, and far happier days.   (II, 464–465)

At this vision Adam is filled with wonder

> That all this good of evil shall produce,
> And evil turn to good;   (II, 470–471)
> ....

Before this fruition can come to pass, though, superstition and secular power will corrupt religion and visit heavy persecution on the conscience of those who seek to worship purely in spirit and truth (XII, 511–533). Michael offers a gloomy picture of the course of secular history:

> so shall the world go on,
> To good malignant, to bad men benign,
> Under her own weight groaning till the day
> Appear of respiration to the just,
> And vengeance to the wicked....   (XII, 537–541)

He completes his account with the Last Judgment, when Christ destroys Satan and his "perverted world," to inaugurate

> New heavens, new earth, ages of endless date
> Founded in righteousness and peace and love
> To bring forth fruits joy and eternal bliss.   (XII, 546–551)

When Michael concludes, Adam expresses profound gratitude for the knowledge communicated to him. The wisdom he has acquired will teach him to love and depend solely on God,

> Merciful over all his works, with good
> Still overcoming evil, and by small
> Accomplishing great things, by things deemed weak
> Subverting worldly strong....   (XII, 565–568)

Taught by the redeemer's example, he has learned

> that suffering for truth's sake
> Is fortitude to highest victory,
> ....   (XII, 569–570)

Praising Adam's response, the archangel assures him that if to his newly won knowledge he adds commensurable deeds – faith, virtue, patience, temperance, and above all love,

> then wilt thou not be loath
> To leave this Paradise, but shalt possess
> A paradise within thee happier far.   (XII, 581–587)

The consolatory knowledge that enables Adam and Eve to depart from Eden with hope for their own and mankind's future is the spiritual culmination of *Paradise Lost*. It seems impossible to doubt that it was also Milton's consolation against the shock and disillusion of the Restoration. This consolation, which comprised both a general human and a political meaning, was not a reflection of Christian otherworldliness. On the contrary, the education the archangel gives Adam after the Fall constitutes a paradigm of the possibilities of development in spiritual understanding and action by individuals which will help to strengthen them in their lives and struggles in the world. The true paradise proves to be one that individual human beings have the means to create within themselves. The reiterated themes of good coming out of evil, of small things accomplishing great, and weakness vanquishing worldly power, may be read as the poet's reconciliation with and transcendence of adversity through trust in divine justice and the ways of providence. His conception of history has become pessimistic, but it is in no way despairing. He knows the tragic defeats the good suffer in this world, and could have pronounced the same words Beethoven wrote above the music of his last quartet, "Muss es sein? Es muss sein." ("Must it be? Yes, it must be.")[15] Yet despite tyranny and violence, the corruption of religion, and the victories of evil evidenced in mankind's repeated failures and transgressions, he can nevertheless regard the order of history as remaining under God's guidance, so that virtuous action and endurance in the defense of truth are never vain and all things turn finally to good.

Paradise Regained, composed between 1667 and 1670, was published in 1671. A brief epic in four books, it was intended as the sequel to *Paradise Lost* and narrates Christ's victory over the temptations Satan sets before him.[16] According to the invocation, the

---

[15] Beethoven placed these sentences at the head of the last movement of his sixteenth quartet in F Major, opus 135.

[16] David Quint, "David's Census: Milton's Politics and *Paradise Regained*," in *Remembering Milton*, discusses some possible political allusions in *Paradise Regained* as

poem will tell how the paradise that Adam's disobedience lost is to be recovered for all mankind by means of

> one man's firm obedience fully tried
> Through all temptation, and the tempter foiled
> In all his wiles, defeated and repulsed,
> And Eden raised in the waste wilderness.   (I, 4–7)

It is evident that like *Paradise Lost*, *Paradise Regained* is also a theodicy, enacting a similar pattern of trial and assurance of victory. In the first epic, Adam and Eve are tempted and fall, but through the knowledge they gain of God's redemptive plan, they can come to terms with their fallen state in the faith that it will be productive of good. In the second epic, Christ represented in his human nature is tempted and overcomes, thus foreshadowing the restitution promised to fallen humanity. The temptations, which with a couple of additions are taken from the gospels of Luke and Mark, occur in the desert while Christ is still in a private station before beginning his public mission. They are tests by which Satan hopes to discover whether he really is the prophesied son of God destined to destroy him. In his encounter with them, Christ performs deeds

> Above heroic, though in secret done,
> And unrecorded left through many an age,
> ....   (I, 15–16)

His heroism, however, consists in endurance and renunciation. He does not engage in action, but manifests his power in a masterly capacity to remain unmoved despite all the allurements with which Satan tries to corrupt him. His posture, nevertheless, is not merely passive, for he replies to Satan's arguments with a mind always conscious of its superiority and at times even haughty in its contemptuous rejection of the tempter. So unshaken is he in his resistance that we may come to wonder whether he even knows temptation. Even so, however, the human Christ of *Paradise Regained* stands as a supreme instance of the self-command to which Milton accorded exemplary significance in morals and politics.

Obedience is one of the main themes of *Paradise Regained*, in some sense even its overarching theme. In the trials he undergoes, it is Christ's obedience to God and his own highest ideals that emerges triumphant. For Milton obedience was related to discipline, a concept emphasized in his earlier prose writings and integral to his

part of his argument that Milton remained a committed republican and opponent of monarchy.

moral and political philosophy. It is probable that the principle of obedience became even more important for him after 1649, as support for the revolution waned and his disappointment with the English people became complete. To obey virtuous men was an attribute of obedience to one's best self. In his eulogy of Cromwell's greatness in the *Second Defence*, he praised the general for first learning how to command and be the victor over himself before he commanded others.[17] *Paradise Regained* includes several episodes that provide occasions for characteristic expressions of the central place the values of discipline, obedience, and self-mastery occupied in his political philosophy.

When Satan offers Jesus wealth as a means to gain greatness and power, he refuses. Neither riches nor realms have any appeal for him, and although acknowledging the virtue of a true king who bears the weight of office for the public good, he holds that

> he who reigns within himself, and rules
> Passions, desires, and fears is more a king;
> Which every wise and virtuous man attains:
> And who attains not, ill aspires to rule
> Cities of men, or headstrong multitudes,
> Subject himself to anarchy within,
> Or lawless passions in him which he serves. (II, 466–472)

For himself he considers it "more kingly still" to reign over the soul, which governs the inner man, and

> to guide nations in the way of truth
> By saving doctrine, and from error lead
> To know, and knowing, worship God aright. (II, 473–477)

The aristocratic ideal of self-conquest is linked to another Miltonic theme, contempt for the people, when Satan, confounded by Jesus' indifference to riches, tempts him with the promise of fame and glory such as Alexander and Caesar possessed. Jesus, however, feels no desire for such things, which are merely the empty products of popular acclaim:

> For what is glory but the blaze of fame,
> The people's praise, if always praise unmixed?
> And what the people but a herd confused,
> A miscellaneous rabble, who extol
> Things vulgar, and well weighed, scarce worth the praise,
> They praise and they admire they know not what.

---

[17] *The Second Defence of The English People*, CPW, vol. IV, pt. 1, p. 668.

> And know not whom, but as one leads the other;
> And what delight to be by such extolled,
> To live upon their tongues and be their talk,
> Of whom to be dispraised were no small praise? (III, 47–56)

Perhaps it seems strange that the future savior of mankind should hold such a low opinion of the common people. We may be sure, though, that it represents the opinion Milton drew from his own political experience.

In place of the false glory bestowed by the popular tongue and won by the slaughter and enslavement of nations (III, 69–76), Jesus seeks a different kind of glory founded in virtue. It is attained

> Without ambition, war or violence;
> By deeds of peace, by wisdom eminent,
> By patience, temperance; (III, 90–92)

To Satan's further urging that he make haste to begin his reign and liberate his nation from heathen servitude, he answers that he waits patiently on God's decree, ready for suffering, tribulation, and humiliation, that God may know how he can suffer and obey. Here it is obedience that Jesus emphasizes as a qualification to rule:

> Who best
> Can suffer, best can do; best reign, who first
> Well hath obeyed; (III, 194–196)

The same ensemble of ideas occurs again in connection with the vision of imperial Rome, "queen of the earth," which Satan shows Jesus with the temptation to make him its emperor who will free the Romans from their tyrannical yoke (IV, 44–45, 97–108). Jesus spurns the offer: the Roman people, "once just, frugal, and mild," have been so deeply corrupted by their conquests, wealth, and luxury that they are no longer capable of freedom (IV, 133–142). "What wise and valiant man," he asks,

> would seek to free
> These thus degenerate, by themselves enslaved,
> Or could of inward slaves make outward free? (IV, 143–145)

In this and previous exchanges touching rule and servitude, Jesus' replies to Satan certify the identical lesson. Milton made no real distinction between morals and politics. Virtue in the individual and in the body politic were inseparable. The individual's failure to govern himself in obedience to justice, temperance, and fortitude ends in self-enslavement. The poet doubtless believed that this conclusion applied to his own countrymen. The impression is unmistakable, though, that his later thought betrays a decreasing concern with political freedom, at least as regards the majority of people, whom he had convicted of incapacity for self-rule. After the Restoration, he seems to have been much more preoccupied with the personal than with the political realm as a vital area of struggle. Only in the soul of the individual could freedom be fought for and won, and only such self-conquest by governors and governed alike could secure the political freedom of the community.

Jesus still faces several more temptations, but he surmounts them all, to Satan's growing fear and consternation. Having thus failed with all his snares, the frustrated devil finally sweeps him up to the highest pinnacle of the Temple in Jerusalem, daring him to stand there on its point if he is the son of God or else fall to his death. To his amazement, Jesus remains firmly standing, while it is he himself who falls (IV, 541–562). This dramatic moment announces Satan's decisive repulse. The poem ends, as it began, with the promise of mankind's restoration. The savior Christ, by vanquishing temptation, has avenged Adam and broken Satan's power (IV, 606–608). The poet speaks directly in his own voice as he binds past and future together in a single encompassing vision. Despite humanity's loss of Eden,

> A fairer Paradise is founded now
> For Adam and his chosen sons, whom thou
> A Savior art come down to reinstate.
> Where they shall dwell secure, when time shall be
> Of tempter and temptation without fear. (IV, 613–617)

With this outcome, Milton confirms once more the working of God's redemptive providence in mankind's behalf. The heroism Christ displays is passive yet positive, consisting in fearlessness and composure of mind, patient endurance, and steadfast fidelity to truth. Like *Paradise Lost*, *Paradise Regained* thus functions as both consolation and sublimation, portraying qualities of heroism that must have had a special meaning for the poet in reconciling himself to the bitter reversal of the Restoration.

Samson Agonistes, a tragic drama intended for reading, not the stage, was published in 1671 in the same volume as *Paradise Regained*. In the absence of definite evidence, scholars have assigned its composition to varying dates, a few arguing that it was written in the later 1640s or in 1660–61. The prevailing opinion, however, has always considered it to be Milton's final work of poetry, composed after

Paradise Regained.[18] Its plot, concentrated within the space of a day, has its main source in the biblical book of Judges. It relates how Samson recovers from the utmost despair caused by his betrayal of God, blindness, and enslavement by the idol-worshipping Philistines, and rises to a height of heroic action in which he brings destruction on the Philistines and himself. Whereas *Paradise Regained* told of a flawless hero who was proof against all temptation, *Samson Agonistes* is again a tale of human failure and its transcendence. It is a drama containing many political overtones, and like the two epic poems that preceded it, it recapitulates the identical pattern of theodicy.

The essential political fact in the drama is the subjection of God's chosen people, Israel, to the heathen Philistines. Samson's personal tragedy is that he is man elected by God for great exploits and the liberation of his people, who has betrayed his high vocation by succumbing to the wiles of his Philistine wife Dalila. Having divulged to her the secret source of his mighty strength, which lies in his long hair, she has shorn him and thus enabled him to be made captive by her countrymen. Blinded by his conquerors and reduced to slavery, tortured by the contrast between what he was and what he has become, he longs for death. The Chorus of Israelites makes clear in its comment that his fall is a fall from virtue, which was the companion of his strength (170–174). Likewise, in recounting former deeds, his own statement affirms the favorite Miltonic doctrine that the subjugation of the Israelites, whose chiefs have collaborated with the Philistines against him, is due to national corruption:

> But what more oft in nations grown corrupt,
> And by their vices brought to servitude,
> Than to love bondage more than liberty,
> Bondage with ease than strenuous liberty; (268–271)

The case of both the hero and his people therefore illustrates the cardinal principle that moral weakness leading to inward enslavement has resulted also in the loss of personal and political freedom.

Samson's process of regeneration begins with his acknowledgement of full responsibility for his failure. Overcoming the temptation to blame God, he accepts that he alone is the author of the evils he is

---

[18] For a discussion of the several dates of composition assigned to the tragedy, see CF, pp. 331–332; Hanford and Taafe, pp. 231–232; John Spencer Hill, *John Milton: Poet, Priest And Prophet* (London: Macmillan, 1979), App.; and Parker, vol. II, pp. 903–910. Christopher Hill, *Milton And The English Revolution* (London: Faber And Faber, 1977), App. 1, and Mary Ann Radzinowicz, *Towards Samson Agonistes*, App. E, defend the majority view of the work's late date.

justly suffering (374–376). He recognizes that the unworthiness of his servitude to Dalila deserved a "servile punishment" (410–414); and he attains the return of a degree of dignity in the firm understanding that the condition of slavery to which he has fallen

> is not yet so base
> As was my former servitude, ignoble,
> Unmanly, ignominious, infamous,
> True slavery, and that blindness worse than this,
> That saw not how degenerately I served. (414–419)

Deeply moved by Samson's plight, the pitying Chorus puts its great question, "God of our fathers, what is man!", which initiates reflections on the justice of God's dealings with his creatures. He strikes down not only the common rout of nameless humanity who perish without memory, but even those he has chosen and adorned with eminent gifts for the advancement of his glory and the safety of the people. Towards these too,

> thou oft
> Amidst their height of noon
> Changest thy countenance, and thy hand with no regard
> Of highest favors past
> From thee on them, or them to thee of service.
>   Nor only dost degrade them, or remit
> To life obscured, which were a fair dismission,
> But throw'st them lower than thou didst exalt them high,
> Unseemly falls in human eye,
> Too grievous for the trespass or omission,
>
> ....

Contemplating the apparent arbitrariness of human destiny, the Chorus feels that

> Just or unjust, alike seem miserable,
> For oft alike, both come to an evil end. (667–704)

This cannot be the drama's ultimate verdict, however, for it ends with the affirmation of God's justice. Samson himself, moreover, is never tempted to entertain the Chorus' opinion, since he regards his fall as deserved.

His moral recovery continues when Dalila appears, seeking forgiveness and hoping to win him back with honeyed promises to love and care for him. Deaf to all her entreaties, however, he hates her and rejects all her excuses for her conduct. After she leaves, the giant Philistine warrior Harapha comes on the scene with taunts that

141

Samson is a murderer and rebel (1178–1180). Samson answers with a justification of the right of rebellion against tyranny:

> My nation was subjected to your lords,
> It was the force of conquest, force with force
> Is well ejected when the conquered can.

Furthermore, he was not a private man in what he did,

> but a person raised
> With strength sufficient and command from heaven
> To free my country; (1205–1213)

These lines convey in a nutshell the essence of Milton's theory of resistance with its religious and political underpinning. Although Samson is blinded and in chains, his hair has grown back during his captivity, and in the name of Israel's God he challenges Harapha to single combat. Not daring to fight him, however, the Philistine stalks off.

The episodes with Dalila and Harapha show that Samson's calamities have not completely destroyed his spirit. His valor and presence of mind in responding to his antagonists testify to his revival from despair. Although he seeks death, expecting it at the hands of the Philistines, we receive an intimation of some possible deed against them (1265–1267). The Chorus also seems to anticipate this possibility when, in an alternative to its earlier view of God's justice, it observes,

> O how comely it is and how reviving
> To the spirits of just men long oppressed!
> When God into the hands of their deliverer
> Puts invincible might
> To quell the mighty of the earth, the oppressor,
> ....
> He all their ammunition
> And feats of war defeats
> With plain heroic magnitude of mind
> And celestial vigor armed
> .... (1268–1280)

The end nears as the Philistines order Samson to appear before them to perform feats of strength at the celebration of the feast of their idol Dagon. At first, despite their threats, he absolutely refuses, determined not to participate in a scene of blasphemy. Then impelled by a sudden inspiration that rises in him, he agrees to go, assuring the Chorus,

> Happen what may, of me expect to hear
> Nothing dishonorable, impure, unworthy
> Our God, our Law, my nation, or myself,
> .... (1423–1425)

What next ensues is told in the report of a messenger. After an incredible display of strength for the Philistine's entertainment, Samson has pulled down the pillars supporting the temple roof, which in its collapse kills all the Philistine nobility and himself. The Chorus hails his act as "dearly-bought revenge, yet glorious;" Samson has accomplished the work for which he was foretold. While in their frenzy and drunk with idolatry and wine, the dissolute Philistines have brought destruction on themselves. The blind hero,

> Despised and thought extinguished quite,
> With inward eyes illuminated
> His fiery virtue roused
> From under ashes into sudden flame,
> has slain his persecutors and will find immortal fame
> (1660–1707).

His father Manoa, who had previously hoped to ransom him from captivity, bids the Chorus not to lament. To Israel Samson has left honor and the chance to regain its freedom if it will.

> Nothing is here for tears, nothing to wail
> Or knock the breast, no weakness, no contempt,
> Dispraise, or blame, nothing but well and fair,
> And what may quiet us in a death so noble. (1708–1724)

The Chorus, in accord with this sentiment, pronounces the conclusion:

> All is best, though we oft doubt,
> What the unsearchable dispose
> Of highest wisdom brings about,
> And ever best found at the close.
> Oft he seems to hide his face,
> But unexpectedly returns
> And to his faithful champion hath in place
> Bore witness gloriously;
> ....
> His servants he with new acquist
> Of true experience from this great event
> With peace and consolation hath dismissed,
> And calm of mind, all passion spent. (1745–1758)

143

Samson Agonistes is thus a renewed declaration of Milton's belief in God's just rule and the reparation of human failure. Probably the tragedy's hatred of the Philistines resembles the poet's animosity to the notorious immorality and corruption of the court of Charles II and the political order of the Restoration. In that sense, the poem may even be a revenge fantasy. Samson's highest heroism appears in his endurance, fortitude, and clarity of mind in accepting responsibility for his sin. Refusing to be crushed by the evils that have befallen him, his moral powers return, and he redeems his virtue by a decisive act of personal resistance to national and religious oppression. That the massacre of the idol-worshipping Philistines is a righteous deed is never in doubt. From the Old Testament standpoint that Milton adopts, they richly deserve their fate as the victims of Samson's ferocious revenge.[19] The drama poses questions about the meaning of history. Milton's answer to them is anchored in his unshaken trust in providence. Contrary to appearances, the course of human affairs is not senseless and indifferent to good and evil. God remains the lord of history, directing events in accord with his often hidden purpose. Although his wisdom is unfathomable, his goodness and justice will be manifest to mankind, as it has been in the case of Samson. This consoling thought, voiced by the Chorus in its concluding lines, is not a warrant for quietism. As always, Milton insists on moral responsibility; he expects the virtuous and godly individual to demonstrate persistence in struggle and endurance against wrong. His final word, nevertheless, is one of faith in the reconciliation between God's designs and the human need for justice, and this assurance was the bedrock of his resistance to the adversities of history.

The last work of any political import from Milton's pen was *Of True Religion, Haeresie, Schism, Toleration*, a short tract published in the spring of 1673. For thirteen years he had avoided controversy until an outburst of anti-Catholic agitation in 1672–73 provided him with a favorable occasion to speak once more. In March 1672, Charles II issued his Declaration of Indulgence suspending the penal statutes

---

[19] The satisfaction the tragedy takes in Samson's revenge should remind us of the call for revenge in Milton's *Sonnet XV* of 1655, "On The Late Massacre in Piedmont," concerning the slaughter of the Protestant Vaudois by the Catholic duke of Savoy, which begins, "Avenge O Lord thy slaughtered saints, whose bones/Lie scattered on the Alpine mountains cold..." As an official of the protectorate's Council of State, Milton drafted letters of protest from Cromwell to various European rulers and a special address to be delivered by the English ambassador to the duke of Savoy himself; see the editorial note in CF, p. 411.

against both Protestant dissenters and Catholics. To the former it granted permission to engage in public worship if they first procured licenses; to the latter, it permitted freedom to worship in private houses. The Declaration, which was based solely on the authority of the royal prerogative, met strong opposition from parliament when it reassembled early in the following year: an opposition springing from both unwillingness to allow liberty to Catholics and the constitutional objection that only parliament had the power to suspend laws. The king in consequence was compelled to withdraw the Declaration. Moreover, parliament passed the Test Act, which required every officeholder to take the Anglican sacrament and disavow the Catholic doctrine of transubstantiation. As a reinforcement of its anti-Catholic stance, the House of Commons also promised to enact a future bill giving relief to Protestant dissenters. These events, which were accompanied by a widespread public outcry against popery, constituted the context of Milton's tract.[20]

Of True Religion was a renewed call for toleration and a fresh denunciation of Catholicism. In pleading again for liberty of conscience, Milton wrote nothing inconsistent with his previous statements on the subject. Nonetheless, he exercised considerable caution in what he said, in particular avoiding all criticism of the government and national church and taking care to use arguments that might appeal to Anglicans as well as dissenters. After defining true religion as the true worship and service of God founded solely on Scripture, he pointed out that all Protestant churches agreed in this principle, including the Church of England in its Thirty-Nine Articles of Religion. If all Protestants fully observed it, he was convinced, they would no longer persecute or quarrel with one another even though they differed in some of their opinions. In contrast with true religion, false religion or heresy consisted in human traditions and additions to the word of God. From this it followed that Catholicism was the greatest if not the only Christian heresy. Error itself was not heresy as long as it proceeded from a sincere desire to understand and follow Scripture as the rule of faith. Hence Milton urged a charitable toleration by Protestants on such disputed subjects as predestination, Arminianism, infant baptism, Arianism, and Socinianism, since none of these doctrines was absolutely necessary to salvation and all those who believed in them

---

20 For the Declaration of Indulgence, its withdrawal, and the Test Act, see J. P. Kenyon, *The Stuart Constitution*, 2nd ed. (Cambridge: Cambridge University Press, 1986), pp. 376, 382–386. Keith W. Stavely's editorial preface to *Of True Religion*, CPW, vol. VIII, pp. 408–413, sketches the tract's historical background.

claimed to find them in Scripture. This meant that every Protestant should be able to express his faith freely, whether in argument, public preaching, or published writings. Milton denied that the civil magistrate had the authority to make commands concerning things indifferent. Such commands were simply additions to Scripture, and what the magistrate deemed indifferent others might regard as an offense against conscience. Thus no one should be required to obey or believe anything in religion save the word of God. Once Protestants accepted this rational and impartial proposition, Milton said, their long contest over whether they should tolerate each other would come to an end.[21]

In the second part of his tract he went on to consider whether Catholicism ("Popery") deserved toleration. Needless to say, the answer he gave was firmly negative. As always, he perceived the Catholic church as a tyrannical institution that had usurped both spiritual and political power. Politically it was highly dangerous because of the papal claim to depose kings and absolve subjects from obedience. Religiously it was guilty of idolatry. For these reasons he held that it would be a scandal to the conscience of believers and an offense to God to tolerate it either publicly or privately. To prevent the growth of popery he recommended the suppression of every trace of Catholic worship. That this would violate the conscience of Catholics he denied, since Protestants had no obligation to respect conscience not grounded on Scripture. As additional measures against popery, he advised the diligent reading of Scripture and full freedom for all Protestants to communicate their beliefs. He was certain that if all controversies were permitted, "falshood will appear more false, and truth the more true: which must needs conduce much...to the confounding of Popery...." Observing lastly that the nation's growth in viciousness in recent years had created a fertile ground for popery, he called for a general amendment in morals. Pride, luxury, drunkenness, whoredom, cursing, and open atheism abounded. Unless people reformed their lives and ceased to sin so outrageously, he warned, God might punish them not only with fire, sword, and pestilence (these were references to the recent great plague and fire of London in 1666), but with popery as well, his heaviest judgment to their final perdition.[22]

Such was Milton's last utterance to his countrymen on public affairs. Written in a plain, dry style lacking the fire or imagery of

---

[21] *Of True Religion*, 1673, CPW, vol. VIII, pp. 417–429.
[22] Ibid., pp. 429–440.

his earlier works, it conveys a sense of tiredness. Its moralistic conclusion, a jeremiad castigating the people's falling away into vice and corruption, reveals his low opinion of Restoration society. His belief in the supreme importance of liberty of conscience remained undimmed, and he had not lost the conviction, voiced nearly thirty years before in *Areopagitica*, that truth was sure to conquer in a free and open contest with falsehood. His hatred of Catholicism continued to be uncompromising. That the individual Catholic conscience might have an equal right to freedom from persecution was beyond his understanding, since he considered it to be tainted at its source. There is no doubt that he approved the Test Act, which made a mockery of the religious conscience by imposing the Anglican sacrament as a loyalty test.

The best that can be said for Milton's attitude on this point is that it did not differ from the one held by most other thoughtful English Protestants of the seventeenth century, including tolerant men such as John Locke, who feared Catholicism as a constant menace.[23] The treaty of Dover in 1670, which allied England with Catholic and absolutist France in a war against the Dutch, contributed to the association in the public mind of Catholicism with arbitrary power that fed this fear. The king's brother, moreover, James duke of York, the heir to the throne, was an open Catholic, and there were also suspicions about Charles II's own religion. Milton's friend and admirer, the poet Andrew Marvell, was a member of the House of Commons for the Yorkshire borough of Hull and may have kept him informed on occasion about developments in parliament. A man of moderate views and an advocate of liberty of conscience, in the 1670s Marvell became convinced of the existence of a conspiracy in the highest quarters to impose Catholicism and absolutism upon England. In his tract of 1678, *An Account of The Growth of Popery And Arbitrary Government*, he voiced opinions similar to Milton's. Refusing to consider popery a religion, he declared that it was not to be mentioned "with that civility which is otherwise decent to be used in speaking of the differences of human opinion about divine matters." He ridiculed its absurd superstitions and impious beliefs, criticized the impostures of its priests under the name of Christianity, and warned of the unreliability of the obedience of Catholic subjects

---

[23] See John Miller, *Popery And Politics in England 1660-1688* (Cambridge: Cambridge University Press, 1973), chaps. 6-7, for an account of anti-Catholic sentiment at this period. G. R. Cragg, *From Puritanism to The Age of Reason* (Cambridge: Cambridge University Press, 1950), chap. IX and pp. 166-168, 204, 218, discusses the unwillingness of Locke, Stillingfleet, and other thinkers to tolerate Catholicism.

because of papal claims to depose kings.[24] Milton's unwillingness to extend toleration to Catholics therefore reflected a widespread Protestant viewpoint. In 1678, increasing apprehension about the growth of popery culminated in the Popish Plot, provoking hysterical fears and a wave of political agitation that rocked Charles II's throne and even appeared to presage a new civil war.

When Milton published *Of True Religion*, he had only a little over a year left to live. During these final months he seems to have tried to prepare his literary legacy. In 1673 he also brought out a collected edition of his shorter poems. The following year saw a second edition of *Paradise Lost* with commendatory verses by Marvell praising his epic's "vast design" and addressing him as "mighty poet." He hoped as well to publish a volume of his collected correspondence, including the letters of state written during his official employment under the commonwealth and protectorate. The government's censor, however, prevented this project, and instead he printed only his familiar letters accompanied by the academic exercises he had composed while a student at Cambridge. His unorthodox beliefs made it impossible for him to publish his treatise on Christian doctrine, which remained unknown for another century and a half. His very last publication during his lifetime was an English translation in 1674 of a Latin declaration announcing the election of John Sobieski as king of Poland.[25] On or about 8 November 1674, Milton died at the age of sixty-five. To posterity he left his work as a poet-prophet and the prose record of his many combats as a revolutionary intellectual, confident that it would accord him the immortal fame which was the goal of his life.

[24] Andrew Marvell, *An Account of The Growth of Popery And Arbitrary Government*, in *Complete Works*, ed. A. B. Grosart, 4 vols. (n. p., 1872–1875), vol. IV, pp. 250–251, 257–258.

[25] Parker, vol. II, surveys these last publications. Marvell's verses are printed in CF, pp. 455–456.

Chapter 6

CONCLUSION

In spite of all the changes he experienced over the years, Milton's life and thought remained essentially unified at their deepest level and exhibited a fundamental consistency. Integrity was the principal note of his personal and intellectual history, and his development contained no severe discontinuities or ruptures. Not even the twenty years of revolution, which he devoted largely to prose rather than to poetry, marked a real break in his evolution. From the beginning to the end of his career a concern with moral or ethical action dominated his work.[1] The great love of beauty, art, and learning that exerted such a power over him was never divorced in his mind from the service of God and the necessity of virtue. Together with vast ambition he possessed immense pride and an extraordinarily strong will and need for control. He refused to admit fissions or divided aims into his personality. If doubts or fears ever threatened him, he always succeeded in negating them so that they failed to undermine his belief in himself and his vocation. His persisting consciousness of election as a divinely-inspired poet-prophet gave shape to his entire life. It animated not only his later epic poems, but the defense of liberty and revolution which he undertook in his prose works. His religious faith was firm and free of skeptical questioning. It was also totally devoid of mysticism. God to him was the sovereign God of goodness, wisdom, and truth to whom love and obedience were due. There is no sign that his relationship with God ever involved a reaching out for communion or the spiritual struggles, the heights and depths, that appear in the religious poetry of Donne or Herbert. He seems always to have felt the assurance of God's presence and favor even in the greatest adversity. More than anything else his religion stressed the moral responsibility of individuals, to whom God, in spite of the Fall, had

[1] The importance of ethics in Milton's politics is also stressed in Charles R. Geisst's study, *The Political Thought of Milton* (London: Macmillan, 1984).

granted freedom of will and reason so that the power of doing right lay in themselves.

Milton's life would have been entirely different if the English revolution had not occurred. Already nearly thirty-two years old in 1640 when the meeting of the Long Parliament initiated the political conflict with the Stuart monarchy, he had still not embarked on a career. Having renounced his long-held intention of entering the ministry, he was simply a scholar supported by his father. It is easy to forget how little he had yet seen of life. Compared to other great writers of his era like Shakespeare, Spenser, Jonson, or Donne, he had lived a sheltered existence. He had no experience of war, of politics, of courts, or of the debasing competition for patronage that some of the poets who were his immediate predecessors or older contemporaries knew at first-hand. Nearly all his knowledge of the world came from books. In the earlier part of Charles I's reign, the court was a major source of patronage for artists and writers, and this would doubtless have continued to be the case if not for the civil war, which put an end to so many things. Although in the 1630s Milton was the author of the two aristocratic entertainments, *Arcades* and *Comus*, it is nevertheless hard to imagine how the austere and idealistic poet could have ever sought affiliation with the sophisticated Caroline court to which he must have felt himself profoundly alien, or produced work that would have appealed strongly to its taste.

The English revolution did more than excite Milton's highest hopes for a great national renewal. It also gave him an urgent, immediate task. If it forced him to defer his project of a great epic poem until after the Restoration, it likewise enabled him to identify himself with a national cause to which he gave his full allegiance and which he felt it his duty to support with his pen. It turned his mind to prose as the medium best suited to the polemical needs of the time in arguing for the issues he had at heart and attacking the views of his opponents. It was in this way that he became a political publicist, throwing himself with heroic energy for twenty years into a succession of controversies in which he declared his strongest commitments as a religious and political rebel.

Liberty and virtue were the determining concepts of Milton's political philosophy. When he looked back in 1654 on the range of his prose writings, he said that all of them sought to advance either ecclesiastical, domestic, or civil liberty, the three kinds of liberty essential to civilized life.[2] Liberty in its several aspects was so

---

[2] *A Second Defence of The English People*, CPW, vol. IV, pt. 1, p. 624.

integrally associated for him with virtue, however, that he could never consider the two apart. With them, moreover, were connected further concepts such as right reason, the law of nature, contract, and consent, which together formed a constellation that defined the character of his political thought.

In his learned and illuminating study, *Milton And The Puritan Dilemma*, Arthur E. Barker saw the poet's Puritanism and theological doctrines as the chief source and determinant of his basic principles. After attempting to trace the complex interrelationship between his religious and other beliefs, Barker concluded that "Christian liberty was...the central theme of Milton's prose."[3] This claim is surely an exaggeration and ascribes to the concept of Christian liberty a much wider importance than it really possessed. Alongside it secular concepts derived from classical moral and political philosophy and European resistance theory were of equal significance in shaping his understanding of liberty. These also exercised a decisive influence in his defense of the right of revolution and the formation of his republicanism. Similarly, his view of virtue was by no means exclusively Christian, but included qualities of character and conduct that were simply human and hence possible to the natural man without the need of supernatural grace.

In his *Christian Doctrine*, Milton gave a chapter to Christian liberty (book I, chap. XXVII), which presents his fullest exposition of its meaning. As he explained it, Christian liberty signified total emancipation from the Mosaic law, which had been abrogated in its entirety by the gospel. Christ had liberated men entirely from its ordinances; and while the Mosaic law was a literal and external law imposed even on those unwilling to receive it, through faith in Christ believers have his law written in their hearts and follow it willingly. One of the main inferences Milton drew from the principle of Christian liberty was that it freed Christians from the judgments of men "and especially from coercion and legislation in religious matters." It also led him to the corollary conviction that the civil magistrate had no authority to compel believers to uniformity, as this would deprive them of the freedom the gospel had given them.[4] Christian liberty was thus a spiritual principle that mandated religious freedom for all believers in Christ. It was less relevant to the political realm except insofar as it prohibited the magistrate from using compulsion to oppress conscience or enforce conformity. Nor

---

[3] Arthur E. Barker, *Milton And The Puritan Dilemma 1641–1660* (Toronto: University of Toronto Press, 1942), pp. 293, 294, 303, 324, 325.

[4] *Christian Doctrine*, CPW, voL. VI, pp. 531–532, 535, 537–538, 541.

did Milton concede it to Catholics, since their church had corrupted the faith in Christ based exclusively on Scripture with the false traditions of men. Its chief function was to provide the main support for Milton's theory of toleration. Throughout his work the rightful claim to Christian liberty underlay all his arguments against the exercise of force in religion, and in his two tracts of 1659, *A Treatise of Civil Power* and *Considerations Touching The Likeliest Means to Remove Hirelings Out of The Church*, it served as the chief justification for his opposition to the state's control of religion and to tithes and other compulsory payments to ministers.

Christian liberty also played an important role in Milton's divorce tracts, where one of his reasons in favor of freedom of divorce for incompatibility of mind and temper held that Christ and the gospel commanded nothing contrary to charity and the good of man. But in urging a right to divorce he appealed in addition to the primordial law of nature, which, because it pertained to human preservation, took precedence over all positive laws. And he also seized upon the analogy between the contracts of marriage and of the people and government to contend that neither of these covenants was binding if opposed to the ends of mutual contentment or freedom for which each was ordained.

Beside Christian liberty, whose greatest office was to protect the conscience of believers from persecution, Milton was no less strongly dedicated to intellectual and political liberty. His arguments in their behalf relied principally on the concepts of reason, the law of nature, and natural right, theoretical principles not dependent on distinctively Christian assumptions. *Areopagitica* was in the largest sense a demand for intellectual liberty as essential to the progress of knowledge and truth. It indicted press censorship as a violation of human reason, insisting that without reason's freedom to know and to choose between good and evil, men could never attain true virtue, which was the product of knowledge, not ignorance. The justification of rebellion and regicide was predicated in part on the doctrines of natural right and the people's original freedom and consent to government. From the proposition that human beings were born free and had instituted governments as a trust subject to conditions, Milton concluded that the people retained their natural right to change and remove their rulers, especially those guilty of tyranny. He also appealed to the normative force of the law of nature for the same purpose. This law, identical with reason, preserved the rights of the people when they subjected themselves to kings and magistrates, and permitted as right and just whatever was done for the common safety.

In his talk of liberty Milton did not strive for analytical clarity or complete consistency. He simply used the term pragmatically in several different senses to argue for the causes in which he believed. What is evident, nevertheless, is that he valued liberty chiefly as a means, not an end. Its nature did not consist for him merely in the absence of restraint or the removal of oppression. First and foremost he conceived it to be an inward possession made visible in a virtuous life. Liberty was therefore good only if subject to reason and used for good and positive ends. Despite his certainty that liberty was mankind's birthright derived from God and the law of nature, he also held that in political society liberty was a privilege that could justly belong to the good alone. As long as he retained his faith in the English people's wisdom and enlightened willingness to follow their leaders in the battle for religious and political emancipation, he perceived no conflict between the freedom of the many and of the select few like himself. As that faith vanished with the disintegration of the Parliamentarian coalition in the later 1640s, however, he became increasingly indifferent to popular freedom and concerned only for the rights of the virtuous minority, even if this meant the permanent subjection of the majority, which had demonstrated its unfitness to be free. Indeed, during the interregnum he was able to maintain by a species of sophistical reasoning that this virtuous minority, the uncorrupted part of the nation, was thus entitled to govern the corrupt majority against its will.

For Milton, accordingly, virtue was an essential qualification for the possession and exercise of civil liberty. From first to last he never departed from the conviction that unless liberty were allied to virtue, it was undeserved and became an evil. It was this insistence on the mutual dependence between liberty and virtue that gave his political philosophy its unvarying aristocratic character. Virtue was likewise one of the most important themes in his reflections upon history, which were largely those of a political moralist. He estimated past societies by the degree to which they were governed by virtuous men. One of the greatest lessons he drew from the study of earlier commonwealths like that of ancient Rome, as well as from the history of his own country, was that whenever leaders and people became corrupted through ambition, power, or excessive wealth, they ceased to be fit for political liberty and were doomed to lose it.

By virtue Milton understood a type of goodness consisting of temperance, wisdom or prudence, fortitude, and justice, natural qualities that figured in both classical and Christian moral philosophy as the four cardinal virtues. These could be equally seen as attributes of right reason, which was closely associated with liberty in his mind. While always insistent that virtue must prove itself in trial and be manifested in a rightly conducted life, he envisaged it as an inward state achieved by self-conquest and discipline. Discipline, another vital principle in his moral and political outlook, did not mean a cruel and repressive tyranny over the self. Milton had a comparatively rounded conception of human personality and its needs. Like Plato, what he sought in the discipline necessary for virtue was an ordering of the self in accordance with right reason, which, by subjecting unruly passions, gave priority to its highest moral capacities.

This was an aristocratic political philosophy because the moral standard it prescribed as the prerequisite for liberty was attainable only by a select few. Despite his theoretical adherence to the doctrine of popular sovereignty, his populism was always limited by his aristocratic orientation, which caused him to care most for the freedom of the virtuous minority. He had no respect for parliaments, the people, or the popular will when he judged that they diverged from the path of virtue and truth. He considered it axiomatic that good government required the rule of the noblest men, and his conception of the function of education emphasized the ideal of aristocratic public service and the training of a select youth for civic leadership in peace and war as its highest aims. Although he conceived of a true aristocracy as one founded on virtue rather than birth, he had no great opinion of the inferior and laboring members of society, whose way of life made virtue remote. From a social standpoint, he thought that the best and wisest men were most likely to originate in the middle rank, which consisted of those diverted neither by luxury and too great wealth nor prevented by want and poverty from achieving the excellence needed for civil government. At the same time, however, he also tended to blur the line between an aristocracy of virtue and of inherited status. Hence he generally expressed respect for eminent descent and worldly nobility, in the belief that those born to high position in society were often likely to receive a superior education and have a spur to virtue in emulating the deeds of noble ancestors.

Milton refused to idealize the English past or look to it for a model of government. Unlike many of parliament's supporters in the civil war, he did not venerate the common law as the source of liberty nor believe in the superiority of the ancient constitution as a polity of immemorial freedom that equally accommodated both the rights of king and people. He was generally critical of custom and tradition both in politics and religion, regarding them for the most part as a sanctification of evil practices and a bar to progress. He would even have done away with the name of parliament as a badge of former

Norman servitude. His political attitude was fundamentally rationalistic. He subscribed to the principles of original freedom and popular sovereignty, the necessity of consent to government, and the people's right to resist and depose kings and magistrates, more because they were consonant with reason and the law of nature than rooted in history.

Following Charles I's execution and the abolition of monarchy in 1649, he became an avowed republican who proclaimed the superiority of republics to other forms of government. His republican ideal, too, possessed a markedly aristocratic character, placing supreme power in a senate composed of the best men who would sit for life. After the revolution of 1688 his writings in defense of regicide, the right of rebellion, and the commonwealth came to occupy an honored place, along with those of Harrington, Sidney, Locke, and others, in the political canon of the radical Whigs and commonwealthsmen of the eighteenth century who were the legatees of the Parliamentarians and republicans of the English revolution.[5]

As we have seen, Milton's republicanism was part of an efflorescence of republican doctrines during the interregnum that found their most significant formulation in the writings of James Harrington.[6] Harrington based his advocacy of a republic on a theory of social change which held that unless the political order as superstructure was in harmony with the balance of property as foundation, a state could not achieve stable government. In England, according to this theory, the decline in the military significance and wealth of the feudal nobility under the early Tudors had resulted in a widepread diffusion of landed property among gentlemen and the people which changed the social basis of power and made a republic an inescapable historical necessity. His model commonwealth combined popular sovereignty with actual rule by an aristocracy of landed gentlemen, the class that he thought had risen to supremacy with the decay of feudalism and which he considered best equipped for the task of governing. Convinced that monarchy was no longer suited to England and could not maintain itself except by force, he felt certain that if a republic possessed the proper institutions to preserve the existing balance of property and insure the common interest, it would be immortal. His political theory, with its master idea of of the balance of property as the necessary foundation of

[5] Caroline Robbins, *The Eighteenth-Century Commonwealthsman* (Cambridge, Mass.: Harvard University Press, 1961), discusses the later Whigs and republicans and the political tradition on which they drew; for Milton, see pp. 5–6, 50–51.

[6] See above, chap. 4.

political power, fascinated contemporary republicans and retained its influence among believers in popular government right down to the end of the eighteenth century.[7]

It is worth noting that John Toland, a republican and freethinker who brought out the first collected edition of Milton's prose in 1698, also published the earliest edition of Harrington's works two years later. As Milton and Harrington were both republicans, it may seem natural to associate the two. They differed considerably in their ideas, however, even though both favored an aristocratic type of republicanism. In his *Readie And Easie Way to Establish A Free Commonwealth*, Milton had criticized various features of Harrington's proposed republic. Harrington, moreover, belonged to a tradition of republican thought to which Milton was much less closely related. This was the tradition of classical republicanism revived by the civic humanism of the Italian Renaissance, of which Machiavelli became the foremost modern representative. Infusing the writings of a number of Florentine thinkers of the fifteenth and earlier sixteenth centuries who turned to the ancient world for inspiration, civic humanism was responsible for giving new life to the classical belief that men were by nature political beings who found their highest fulfillment through participation as citizens in a self-governing commonwealth. It was devoid of any notion of natural rights, original freedom, the law of nature, or a contract of government. It did not conceive of virtue primarily in ethical terms but as dependent on civic membership and the citizen's willingness to subordinate his private interests to the public good and the preservation of the state.[8] In the case of Machiavelli, the concept of *virtù* he set forth in his two principal works, *The Prince* and *Discourses on The First Decade of Livy*, was a radical departure from the meaning of virtue as understood by classical and Christian philosophers. Deeply preoccupied with the effect of fortune in wrecking the schemes of men, the *virtù* he recommended to rulers and politicians was intended to equip them to withstand and triumph over fortune's power in human affairs. Its nature

---

[7] See Perez Zagorin, *A History of Political Thought in The English Revolution* (London: Routledge & Kegan Paul, 1954), chap. XI, and J. G. Pocock's introduction to *The Political Works of James Harrington* (Cambridge: Cambridge University Press, 1977), for a discussion of Harrington's political theory and its subsequent influence.

[8] J. G. Pocock, *The Machiavellian Moment. Florentine Political Thought And the Atlantic Republican Tradition* (Princeton: Princeton University Press, 1975) contains a detailed and penetrating discussion of this tradition of classical republicanism associated with civic humanism and of Harrington's relationship to it. He does not include Milton within it.

combined cunning, dissimulation, flexibility, and boldness of spirit that could adapt themselves to any and all circumstances in order to gain power or preserve the state. One of its essential attributes was the ability to ignore the rules of morality and to lie, cheat, break promises, and kill when necessity dictated.[9]

Together with Thomas Hobbes, Machiavelli exerted the strongest influence on Harrington's work. To the Italian writer, whom he praised as the restorer of the ancient prudence of republican Rome, he owed some the main tenets of his republicanism, including the belief that a free state must be defended by citizen soldiers, not by mercenaries. From the English philosopher, whose greatness he recognized, he took the mechanistic and deterministic concepts that led him to look for demonstrable causal principles on which to base the political order. Milton, by contrast, was far removed from either of these two thinkers. The Bible, Plato, and Cicero influenced his political philosophy much more than any modern authors. Although he had studied several of Machiavelli's works, especially the *Discourses on The First Decade of Livy*, his republicanism bears no distinctive trace of the Italian's influence.[10] As for Hobbes, Milton disliked his politics and ignored his work altogether in his own writings.[11] Unlike the republicanism of the civic humanist tradition, Milton did not view virtue chiefly in a political context or ascribe a great deal of importance to the citizen's participation in the *res publica*. It goes without saying that he would have completely rejected both Machiavelli's

[9] Pocock's *The Machiavellian Moment*, includes a discussion of the concept of virtue in Machiavelli and early modern republicanism; Quentin Skinner, *Machiavelli* (New York: Hill And Wang, 1981) gives a perceptive account of the meaning of Machiavelli's *virtù*.

[10] In his *Commonplace Book*, Milton referred almost twenty times to Machiavelli, especially to his *Discourses*; see CPW, vol. I, p. 414n. The editor has tentatively assigned some of these notes to 1651–52, but their dates must remain uncertain. One entry quoted *The Art of War* to the effect that a republic is superior to monarchy because it contains more excellent men and honors virtue more; ibid., p. 421. Although it seems likely that Milton would also have known *The Prince*, the *Commonplace Book* does not mention it. Alluding to these notes, Blair Worden has inferred from them a much greater importance of Machiavelli in the formation of Milton's republicanism than is justified; "Milton's Republicanism And The Tyranny of Heaven," in *Machiavelli And Republicanism*, ed. Gisela Bock, Quentin Skinner, Maurizio Viroli (Cambridge: Cambridge: Cambridge University Press, 1990, pp. 232–233). See also Felix Raab's discussion in *The English Face of Machiavelli* (London: Routledge & Kegan Paul, 1964), pp. 175–180, which holds that the Italian thinker exercised no direct influence on Milton's republicanism.

[11] See John Aubrey, *Brief Lives*, ed. Andrew Clark, 2 vols. (Oxford, 1898), vol. II, p. 72, who reports Milton's dislike of Hobbes' ideas.

political amoralism and his claim that the virtues inculcated by Christianity were antithetical to those required by republican citizenship. He recognized no distinction between the good man and the good citizen or politician. The corruption he feared most as the cause of political decline and the loss of liberty was the subversion of the moral character of the individual. Virtue, the source of inner freedom, lay in personal self-mastery and obedience to right reason. Nothing seemed more certain to him than that a nation whose leaders and people lacked virtue in this sense were unfitted for political liberty.[12]

Although Milton's contribution to political thought is over-shadowed by his work as an artist, his political ideas possess a lasting interest because he was the first great English poet who also became a committed revolutionary. Whereas his literary prede-cessors nearly always aligned themselves with the wielders of power, the kings, courts, and nobility whose patronage they solicited, Milton chose the side of rebellion and made himself part of all the insurgent forces of his age. To this choice he held consistently throughout the twenty years of the English revolu-tion. Nothing he wrote in the years following the Restoration indicates that he ever regretted his faithful support of the commonwealth or republicanism. He was never subservient to a party nor a captive to any orthodoxy, remaining always a supreme individualist whose position resists easy definition.[13] A fearless spirit of revolt and questioning is apparent in all of his political writings. His loyalty to the principle of liberty as he understood it was absolute. His strenuous conception of virtue and insistence on the individuals' moral responsibility in the tests of living stand as a permanent challenge to conformity and cowardice. He could have said with Goethe,

> Das ist der Weisheit letzter Schluss:
> Nur der verdient sich Freiheit...
> Der täglich sie erobern muss.[14]

---

[12] Jonathan Scott, *Algernon Sidney And The English Republic, 1623–1677* (Cambridge: Cambridge University Press, 1988), chap. 2, examines Milton's differences from the civic humanist republican tradition represented by Harrington and Machiavelli.

[13] See Joseph H. Summers' perceptive essay, "Milton And The Cult of Conformity," in *Milton: Modern Judgments*, ed. Alan Rudrum (London: Macmillan, 1968).

[14] "This is wisdom's final word: /Only he is deserving of freedom.../Who daily conquers it anew." J. W. Goethe, *Faust, Part 2*, V, 2, ll. 25–27.

He was second to none in his time in his independence, his moral and intellectual courage, and his devotion to the cause of freedom of conscience. In spite of shortcomings, errors, illusions, and the lapses of which he was guilty in controversy, Milton was a heroic figure whose greatness of personality is no less manifest in his political life than in his achievement as a poet.

INDEX